THE MEXICAN STATES OF OAXACA AND PUEBLA

showing localities
mentioned in the text

km

0   25   50   75   100

N

OAXACA

Nejapa

Guevea   Juchitán

Guiengola

Tehuantepec

Ocelotepec

Pacific Ocean

THE CLOUD PEOPLE
Divergent Evolution of the Zapotec and Mixtec Civilizations

A School of American Research Book

THE CLOUD PEOPLE

Divergent Evolution
of the Zapotec and Mixtec Civilizations

EDITED BY

Kent V. Flannery
Joyce Marcus

Museum of Anthropology
University of Michigan
Ann Arbor, Michigan

1983

ACADEMIC PRESS
A Subsidiary of Harcourt Brace Jovanovich, Publishers
New York   London
Paris   San Diego   San Francisco   São Paulo   Sydney   Tokyo   Toronto

ACADEMIC PRESS, INC.
111 Fifth Avenue, New York, New York 10003

United Kingdom Edition published by
ACADEMIC PRESS, INC. (LONDON) LTD.
24/28 Oval Road, London NW1 7DX

Library of Congress Cataloging in Publication Data

Main entry under title:

The Cloud people.

  Includes index.
  1. Zapotec Indians--Antiquities--Addresses, essays,
lectures. 2. Mixtec Indians--Antiquities--Addresses,
essays, lectures. 3. Indians of Mexico--Oaxaca Valley--
Antiquities--Addresses, essays, lectures. 4. Oaxaca
Valley (Mexico)--Antiquities--Addresses, essays,
lectures. 5. Mexico--Antiquities--Addresses, essays,
lectures. I. Flannery, Kent V. II. Marcus, Joyce.
F1219.8.Z39C56 1982   972'.74   82-16464
ISBN 0-12-259860-1

PRINTED IN THE UNITED STATES OF AMERICA

83 84 85 86   9 8 7 6 5 4 3 2 1

For his pioneering work on the archaeology and ethnohistory of the Cloud People—enumerated on the pages that follow—the members of the seminar have affectionately dedicated this volume to

IGNACIO BERNAL

Contents

3   The Formative Village and the Roots of Divergence

4   The Origins of the State in Oaxaca

5   The Early Urban Period

6   Monte Albán and Teotihuacán

7   The Changing Politics of A.D. 600–900

8 The Postclassic Balkanization of Oaxaca

Section 8b   The Zapotec Response to Mixtec and Aztec Power

9   Mixtec and Zapotec at the Time of the Spanish Conquest: Some Similarities and Differences

10   Summary and Conclusions

Contributors

Numbers in parentheses indicate the pages on which the authors' contributions begin.

Richard E. Blanton (83, 128, 166, 186, 281, 318), Department of Sociology and Anthropology, Purdue University, West Lafayette, Indiana 47907

Robert D. Drennan (30, 46, 65, 110, 190, 207, 288, 363), Department of Anthropology, University of Pittsburgh, Pittsburgh, Pennsylvania 15260

Eva Fisch (50), Department of Anthropology, Hunter College of the City University of New York, New York, New York 10021

Kent V. Flannery (1, 18, 20, 26, 32, 36, 43, 50, 53, 65, 74, 87, 99, 102, 111, 123, 132, 158, 181, 204, 206, 214, 217, 277, 289, 290, 295, 318, 323, 339, 361), Museum of Anthropology, University of Michigan, Ann Arbor, Michigan 48109

Joseph W. Hopkins (13, 266), 3904 Greenmount Avenue, Baltimore, Maryland 21218

Stephen A. Kowalewski (50, 96, 109, 148, 168, 188, 285), Department of Anthropology, University of Georgia, Athens, Georgia 30602

Joyce Marcus (4, 36, 42, 53, 74, 87, 91, 106, 111, 113, 123, 125, 137, 144, 150, 158, 175, 181, 191, 204, 214, 217, 277, 282, 289, 295, 301, 314, 345, 355), Museum of Anthropology, University of Michigan, Ann Arbor, Michigan 48109

Christopher L. Moser (211, 270), Riverside Municipal Museum, Riverside, California 92501

John Paddock (98, 115, 170, 186, 197, 208, 272, 308, 351), Centro de Estudios Oaxaqueños, Oaxaca, Oaxaca, Mexico

Elsa M. Redmond (71, 117), Department of Anthropology, University of Connecticut, Storrs, Connecticut 06268

Donald Robertson (105, 131, 167, 213, 245), Department of Art, Newcomb College of Tulane University, New Orleans, Louisiana 70118

Mary Elizabeth Smith (213, 238, 248, 260), Department of Art, University of New Mexico, Albuquerque, New Mexico 87131

C. Earle Smith, Jr. (13, 206), Department of Anthropology, University of Alabama, University, Alabama 35486

Charles S. Spencer (71, 117), Department of Anthropology, University of Connecticut, Storrs, Connecticut 06268

Ronald Spores (20, 36, 46, 72, 77, 120, 152, 155, 207, 227, 246, 255, 339, 342), Department of Sociology and Anthropology, Vanderbilt University, Nashville, Tennessee 37235

Preface

An advanced seminar entitled "The Cloud People: Evolution of the Zapotec and Mixtec Civilizations of Oaxaca, Mexico" was held 6–10 October 1975 at the School of American Research in Santa Fe, New Mexico. On the advice of the school's director, Douglas W. Schwartz, the working group invited was held to 10 persons: Ignacio Bernal of the Instituto Nacional de Antropología e Historia, Mexico, Richard E. Blanton, Robert D. Drennan, Kent V. Flannery, Stephen Kowalewski, Joyce Marcus, John Paddock, Donald Robertson, Mary Elizabeth Smith, and Ronald Spores. At the last moment, Dr. Bernal, to whom this volume is dedicated, was unable to attend.

Because the format of this seminar was somewhat different from that of the usual archaeological conference, let us begin with a few words of explanation. This volume is in no sense a synthesis of or textbook on the archaeology of Oaxaca, nor is it a synthesis of or textbook on the Zapotec and Mixtec. Rather, it is a case study in divergent evolution.

As outlined in Chapter 1, divergent evolution is the process by which contrasting cultures evolve from a common ancestor. It may include such processes as adaptive radiation, by which daughter cultures master a series of specific environmental settings to which they become uniquely well suited. It may also include nonadaptive divergence or "drift," where changes in daughter cultures occur as a result of partial isolation from each other, rather than for specifically adaptive reasons. It may also include changes that are the result of diffusion or acculturation from neighboring cultures, or from renewed contact with another daughter culture after a period of isolation. We selected the Cloud People—the Zapotec of the Valley of Oaxaca and the Mixtec of the Mixteca Alta—because their archaeological record shows examples of all these processes. By the same token, we have left aside the Sierra and Isthmus Zapotec, the Mixtec of the Baja and Costa, and such other Oaxacan peoples as the Chatino, Trique, Amuzgo, and Chinantec, because so little was known of their prehistory in 1975.

Our first step was to identify the common ancestral culture from which the Zapotec and Mixtec evolved. It is a step that the historical linguists of the past three decades had already taken. According to glottochronological data, prior to 5000 B.C. one common language—called *Proto-Otomanguean* for convenience—was spoken by the linguistic ancestors of the Otomí, Pame, Chinantec, Mixtec, Cuicatec, Zapotec, Chatino, and their relatives. Sometime between 4100 and 3700 B.C., the speakers of a language ancestral to Zapotec and Chatino became sufficiently separated from the speakers of a language ancestral to Mixtec and Cuicatec so the two began to drift apart linguistically. This may be considered the first of many divergences of the Indian groups with which our seminar was concerned.

The ancestors of the historic Mixtec, separated from the ancestors of the historic Zapotec, adapted to a set of small, high-altitude valleys, and evolved their own special brand of *cacicazgo* political organization; they were significantly influenced by the early Classic state at Monte Albán to the south, then later by the Postclassic Toltec and Aztec states to the north. The ancestors of the historic Zapotec adapted to one large, interconnected valley system and evolved a somewhat different brand of centralized, militaristic state; they were affected by a "special relationship" with Classic Teotihuacán, then later significantly influenced by the expansionist Postclassic Mixtec and Aztec. In turn, both these remarkable Oaxacan people had their own profound effects on their neighbors in the fields of writing, calendrics, military organization, architecture, and urban life.

In A.D. 1520, the two cultures the Spanish chroniclers called Zapotec and Mixtec were the products, not only of their sixteenth-century adaptation, but of their 10,000-year histories as well. In examining the Mixtec and Zapotec cultures of this era, one sees a number of cultural similarities and differences that owe their origins to these histories. Of the similarities they show, some are a legacy of their common origin in the Preceramic cultures of the southern Mexican highlands; others are a result of convergence during the period of Postclassic royal intermarriage; still others are the product of parallel evolution over hundreds of years. Of the differences they show, some are a legacy of the Formative period when each culture was adapting its agricultural and settlement systems to contrasting valleys; some are the result of centuries of partial isolation; others reflect the very different kinds of political organization the two peoples evolved. Still other contrasts result from the differential influence of Nahua peoples on the Mixtec, and of Isthmian and Chiapas peoples on the Zapotec. As we argue at the end of the volume, one could not hope to explain very many of the similarities and differences between the Zapotec and Mixtec without taking their history into account.

This theoretical framework obviously influenced our choice of participants in the Santa Fe seminar. We needed people who knew Oaxacan prehistory, and whose minds also would be open to an approach featuring divergent evolution or adaptive radiation. At the same time, we did not want our use of this explicitly ecological–evolutionary model to degenerate into the kind of monolithic cultural materialism that has characterized some archaeological theory in recent years. We did not want simply a description of how the Cloud People adapted their technology, farming, and economic networks to their respective valleys, or how they responded to demographic changes. We wanted people who were also willing to dig for the ancient cosmology, ethnoscience, ritual, religion, writing, and metaphysics of the Mixtec and Zapotec, regardless of the effort required. Because our format demanded intercultural comparison, we also wanted people who knew more than one area of Mesoamerica, people who could tell us how the Cloud People differed from the Aztec, the Maya, the Olmec, the Teotihuacanos, or the people of Tehuacán.

We also wanted people who were willing to work hard. We prepared an agenda with 68 topics, beginning with "The Common Origin of the Zapotec and Mixtec" and ending with "The National Character of the Sixteenth-Century Zapotec and Mixtec." Covered in chronological order over the 5-day seminar, these 68 topics were designed to document the divergent evolution of the Cloud People from 10,000 B.C. to A.D. 1580. And our participants did not have a choice of topic; rather, each participant was assigned all those topics we believed he or she knew something about. Participants who were listed for five or six topics considered themselves lucky when they learned that John Paddock had been assigned a total of 16. Neither he nor they ever complained.

A few hours into the seminar, we knew we had the people we needed. Blanton and Kowalewski had the only intensive settlement survey results for the Valley of Oaxaca, Spores the only comparable data from the Mixteca, and Drennan the only survey data from the mountains in between. Because of his previous work in the Valley of Mexico, Blanton was prepared to compare the settlement data from that area with his surveys in Oaxaca, and to contrast urban Monte Albán with Teotihuacán. Robertson, an ex-

pert on Precolumbian architecture and city planning, showed us how the buildings of those great cities diverged from ancestral prototypes. Smith and Marcus between them were able to contrast Mixtec, Zapotec, Aztec, and Maya writing. Paddock, who had excavated in the "Zapotec barrio" at Teotihuacán, as well as in both the Mixteca and the Valley of Oaxaca, shared with us the insights of more than 20 years of fieldwork. Drennan and Flannery, both having worked in Tehuacán, attempted to put Preceramic and Formative Oaxaca into perspective with MacNeish's earlier work. Ethnohistorians Spores, Smith, and Paddock inspired Marcus and Flannery to submerge themselves in a new world of sixteenth-century *lienzos* and *relaciones* as the seminar worked its way up to the historic Mixtec and Zapotec.

Nine persons seemed like an ideal group, although there were times when we wished for the advice of someone who was not there. Time and again we missed Bernal, who would have been our link to the original excavations at Monte Albán. We had decided not to cover the Oaxaca coast, but inevitably questions arose that might have been answered by Donald Brockington, or Robert and Judith Zeitlin. We had originally decided not to cover the Cuicatec Cañada, which lies between Tehuacán and Oaxaca, but found that we had questions for Jody Hopkins, Charles Spencer, Elsa Redmond, and Gilberto Hernández. We had decided not to cover the Mixteca Baja, but missed Chris Moser. And constantly we felt the need for a good Oaxacan linguist like Kenneth Pike, Velma Pickett, or Robert MacLaury.

In the end, we wound up with an even 100 topics, having dropped some, added others, and included a few papers from colleagues not actually at the seminar. Where necessary, the editors have prepared additional selections from the literature to fill gaps perceived in the volume, or to cover topics no one else wanted. The 30 hours of tape recordings of the conference were used to design editorial introductions for each of the major sections of the book, and although we have tried for a consensus, these introductions do not necessarily reflect the opinions of all the participants.

In selecting a title for this book, we have followed a long-established Oaxaca tradition. According to this tradition, both the Zapotec and Mixtec referred to themselves as the Cloud People (Zapotec *Ben-Zaa*, Mixtec *Ñusabi*), supposedly a reflection of their common ancestry. There are some objections to this tradition: for example, today's Sierra Zapotec refer to themselves simply as *gente del Rincón*, and some linguists believe that the Valley Zapotec expression *ben-za* may simply mean "our people." The Mixtec, according to some ethnohistorians, saw themselves as having descended from trees or arisen from the ground, rather than from clouds.

There would seem to be little doubt that the sixteenth-century Valley Zapotec called themselves *peni-zaa*, "Cloud People" (Córdova 1578a) because they themselves informed the Spaniards that the *zaa* referred to ancestral clouds (which they sometimes pictured as flying turtles). Even today, the Juchitán Zapotec refer to their ancestors as *binigulaza,* "old people of the clouds." The Aztecs however, "made a phonetic rather than a semantic translation" of the *zaa,* resulting in *Zapotecatl.*

According to the Aztec, the Mixtec lived in Mixtlan, "the place of clouds," from which the Spaniards took them to be "Cloud People" as well. But the Mixtecs' term for themselves, *Ñusabi,* does not even include the sixteenth-century

Mixtec term for "cloud," *huico* (Alvarado 1593). We suspect that *Ñusabi* must be a faulty transcription of *ñuu-dzavui,* "people of Rain," a reference to the most powerful supernatural recognized by the Mixtec (Smith, Topic 71).

In short, if the tradition of the Cloud People is a myth, it is a myth we can attribute to the sixteenth-century Aztecs and Spaniards. There are already so many disillusionments and shattered myths in this volume, however, that we have decided the Cloud People is one tradition we shall maintain.

Acknowledgments

A great deal of the research reported here is a product of the past 17 years, and the authors would like to take this opportunity to thank the various granting agencies involved. Flannery, Blanton, Spores, Drennan, and Spencer were supported by the National Science Foundation; Marcus by the National Endowment for the Humanities; Redmond by Yale University and the Wenner–Gren Foundation for Anthropological Research. Smith acknowledges a Phillips Fund grant from the American Philosophical Society and a travel grant from the University of New Mexico. Spores received grants from the Vanderbilt University Center for Latin American Studies and the Vanderbilt University Research Council. Blanton acknowledges the Research Foundation of the City University of New York. Paddock received support from the Athwin Foundation and the University of the Americas, and Kowalewski was funded by a gift to the University of Arizona. Without the aid of those institutions, this volume would never have been possible. Nor would it have been possible without the kind permission of Mexico's Instituto Nacional de Antropología e Historia and especially Manuel Esparza, director of the Centro Regional de Oaxaca.

We are indebted to a series of talented artists who illustrated the volume, among them Margaret Van Bolt, Mark Orsen, F. E. Smiley, Caren Walt, Katherine Clahassey, Nancy Hansen, Lisa Klofkorn, Lois Martin, and Jane Mariouw. And our unwieldy manuscript would never have become a book were it not for the dedication of the editors and staff at Academic Press.

We would also like to thank Dr. and Mrs. Douglas Schwartz, Mrs. Ella Schroeder, David Noble, and Dr. and Mrs. Philip L. Schultz for their hospitality while we were in Santa Fe. We are pleased to single out two young women—Diana Wimett and Kathy Wigley—who turned our Santa Fe kitchen into a gourmet paradise for 5 consecutive days. Archaeologists who work hard also like to play hard, and we enjoyed our occasional diversions: the quiet beauty of Bandelier National Monument, the autumn breeze off the Sierra just at sunset, and the little old white refrigerator that never seemed to run out of beer. Well, hardly ever. On one memorable evening, eight people wiped out three cases of Coors (Betsy Smith earned the new Mesoamerican calendric name "Lady 9 Can"), and we were driven to Santa Fe's noisiest bar to watch Monday Night Football. All we can remember from that point on is that somehow Don Robertson's sense of decorum was offended by Howard Cosell's remark, "I've never seen the Cowboys' split end so wide open." No wonder everyone who's ever spent 5 days at the School of American Research racks his brain to come up with an idea for another seminar.

Contributions of Ignacio Bernal
to the Study of the Zapotec and Mixtec: A Minimal Survey

Compiled by John Paddock and Kent V. Flannery

1941–1942
1942–1943 } Bernal works three winter seasons excavating at Monte Albán.
1943–1944

1945   Bernal begins regular work with Caso in the San Ángel laboratory on what is then conceived as "the final report on Monte Albán"; he takes responsibility for revision of preliminary reports on early Monte Albán ceramics.

1946   Bernal presents his Master's thesis at the Escuela Nacional de Antropología e Historia, "La cerámica preclásica de Monte Albán," on the pottery of Periods I and II. This study includes the definitive descriptions of the G, C, K, and A wares, the descriptions of their early types, and an internal chronology of Period I (Ia, Ib, Ic.)

1947   Bernal's first technical publication ("Los calendarios de Durán," *Revista Mexicana de Estudios Antropológicos* IX, 125–134) reveals some important traits of future work: profound interest in historical sources, fascination with Aztec archaeology and ethnohistory, penetrating clarity in stating complex questions and defining their implications. (As a grandson of the great Mexican historiographer Joaquín García Icazbalceta, Bernal had been given since childhood a favorable attitude toward research in Mexican history by his mother, Rafaela García Pimentel, a forceful and brilliant woman.)

1948   Bernal excavates at Coixtlahuaca in the Mixteca Alta. This is the first effective combination of archaeology and ethnohistory in Oaxaca, achieving archaeological confirmation of some implications perceived in Aztec chronicles, but also giving new insights into late non-Aztec Mesoamerica.

1949   In his doctoral thesis presented at the Universidad Nacional Autónoma de México, "La cerámica de Monte Albán IIIa," Bernal gives a definitive report on one important aspect of Monte Albán archaeology, later incorporated into the overall publication on Monte Albán ceramics.

1951   On the death of Robert H. Barlow, Bernal becomes chairman of the Anthropology Department at Mexico City College, where he guides students toward Oaxaca research.

1952   Directing a group of Mexico City College students, Bernal excavates sites, including Yatachío, at Tamazulapan, Oaxaca. Once again, the research design combines ethnohistory and archaeology; it is also planned to illuminate the role of the Tamazulapan Valley in relation to the major Mixteca center of Coixtlahuaca.

1952   *Urnas de Oaxaca*, of which Bernal is junior author (with Alfonso Caso) is published as the first volume in a series of major works planned to constitute the final report on Monte Albán. This volume analyzes Oaxaca "urns" to provide data on ancient Oaxaca religion, appealing to both archaeological and ethnohistorical data, while simultaneously providing developmental and chronological conclusions.

1952   Attempting once again to combine ethnohistoric and archaeological research, Bernal begins excavations at Zaachila with a group of Mexico City College students. After only 2 hours' work, he is forced to stop; but before departing in a shower of stones, he insists on staying through a speech by the local mayor, who attempts to persuade a hostile local faction to allow the work.

1953   Frustrated at Zaachila, Bernal takes his students to Macuilxochitl, another site prominent in early chronicles, and accomplishes minor excavations there. During this same season he also uses the student help in beginning a survey of Valley of Oaxaca sites, as well as excavating Tomb 172 at Monte Albán (which was provided with a glass door so that visitors may see it as it was found).

1954   Again with students, Bernal excavates at Cuilapan, failing to find confirmation of early chronicles; later he learns that they are confirmed, but at a nearby site. In the same season, he begins work at Yagul—not because of any chronicled data, but as the probable source of a large looted collection in Tlacolula. Primarily because of its superabundance of Monte Albán V materials, so scanty at Monte Albán itself, the Yagul work continues—at times without Bernal—until 1961, with the aid of Gamio, Paddock, and Wicke. Also during this season, further sites are added to the survey.

1955–1956   Bernal serves in France as cultural attaché of the embassy and delegate to UNESCO.

ca. 1957   Determined to elucidate the end of Monte Albán, Bernal seeks out sites apparently occupied around the time of its decline. One of these, Noriega, is promising also because it lies between Cuilapan, chronicled as a major Mixtec center, and Zaachila, chronicled as the major contemporary Zapotec capital. Noriega does fall into the desired time span, but its excavation does not produce the desired result.

1958   Still looking for what Noriega failed to provide, Bernal works at San Luis Beltrán, a larger site dating to the time of Monte Albán's decline and virtual abandonment. Once again, the study fails to provide the desired explanations.

1958	Determined to locate a site that will illuminate better the end of Monte Albán, and at the same time to achieve a fuller understanding of many aspects of Valley of Oaxaca culture history, Bernal makes the survey of valley sites into a real campaign, with the aid of Lorenzo Gamio. This settlement pattern survey is the first attempted in the southern Mexican highlands and remains one of the most ambitious surveys ever attempted in Mesoamerica, especially given the extreme limitation of human (and other) resources. By 1960, over 200 sites having at least one apparently pyramidal mound have been located and dated in the Etla, Zaachila–Zimatlán, Ocotlán, Ejutla, and Tlacolula sectors of the central valleys. Only the Ejutla–Miahuatlán sector is less fully covered, because of increasing administrative responsibilities that restrict Bernal more to the national capital.
1961	At Mitla, Bernal executes still another study that successfully combines archaeology with ethnohistory.
1962	Bernal publishes his monumental *Bibliografía de Arqueología y Etnografía: Mesoamérica y Norte de México, 1514–1950.* Ironically, in order to finish this work, he found it necessary to seek a visiting professorship at the University of Texas to use the library (long installed at Austin) of his own grandfather (García Icazbalceta); in addition, he received an appointment at Harvard to use its libraries. There are 564 references on Oaxaca alone among the well over 30,000 variously indexed entries.
1963–1964	As director of a gigantic government cleanup and excavation at Teotihuacán, and as a major planner of the Museo Nacional de Antropología, technical adviser for the Oaxaca Room, and finally director of the Museo, Bernal is temporarily unable to work in Oaxaca.
1966	Planning to spend a couple of days uncovering a partially exposed carved stone discovered by his survey, Bernal begins work at Dainzú. The stone is revealed to be only one of dozens; the site is continuous with the Macuilxochitl site and thus is an extremely large community apparently occupied at least from Monte Albán I until the Conquest; but the sector most thoroughly studied is principally a Monte Albán II administrative center, with a Period V ballcourt and an important Period IIIa tomb.
1967	With Alfonso Caso and Jorge R. Acosta, Bernal publishes *La Cerámica de Monte Albán,* one of the most comprehensive, well-illustrated, and workable studies of ceramics ever produced for Precolumbian America. This enormous volume is the second of the planned series on Monte Albán. (Caso's report on Tomb 7, in 1969, was to be the third.)
1968–1971	Bernal's fieldwork is interrupted by his appointment as director of the Instituto Nacional de Antropología e Historia.
1971	Following Caso's death in 1970, Bernal increases the tempo of work on his catalog of the carved stones in the valley. Many previously unknown ones had been added to the list during the years of Bernal's site survey, as an eventual complement to Caso's 1928 book, *Las*

Estelas Zapotecas. By 1973 he has published those of the Tlacocha-huaya–Dainzú–Macuilxochitl–Teotitlán area, and in 1974 a group of stone reliefs in the Frissell Museum at Mitla.

1974   With Lorenzo Gamio, Bernal publishes *Yagul: El Palacio de los Seis Patios,* the first major monograph—again a model of abundant, useful illustration—on a Monte Albán V administrative center.

1977– present   Retiring from his post as director of the Museo Nacional de Antropología, Bernal plunges at once into an intense program of writing, much of it on Oaxacan topics, for professional and trade publishers and for the Academia Nacional de la Lengua, the Academia Mexicana de la Historia, and El Colegio Nacional.

Theoretical Framework

TOPIC 1
Divergent Evolution

KENT V. FLANNERY

If ever there was a long-lived concern within the field of anthropology, it is cultural evolution. And if ever there was a subfield of anthropology uniquely suited to the study of evolution, it is archaeology. One hundred years after Lewis H. Morgan, the evolution of ancient society remains an evergreen research problem that apparently troubles the sleep both of those archaeologists who believe in it and those who do not.

By its briefest definition, evolution is simply "descent with modification": successive generations of organisms diverge progressively from their ancestors. This divergence may be adaptive, as in the oft-cited case of the peppered moth populations that went from predominantly white to predominantly gray as the trees that provided their camouflage were darkened by the industrial revolution in the British Midlands. Alternatively, it may be the result of nonadaptive divergence or "drift," made possible by a degree of isolation from related populations. Over four decades ago, Sewall Wright (1939) argued that the most favorable conditions for biological evolution were to be found in a large species divided into numerous local races: the partial isolation of each race made the fixing of favorable new adaptations rapid, while their partial interaction increased the likelihood that such an innovation would ultimately draw the whole species up to a new adaptive plateau.

It is not our purpose here to pursue another tiresome biological analogy, so let us proceed immediately to cultural evolution. Here the simple process of descent with modification has been called "specific evolution" (Sahlins and Service 1960), and it refers to the pathway taken by a given human culture through time. Partly through adaptive change, partly through isolating mechanisms and drift, part-

ly through the influence of their neighbors, specific cultures play out a history of multigenerational evolution. But this is not the type of evolution that kindled so much interest and controversy in the 1950s and 1960s.

It was another kind of evolution—"general evolution"—that excited Julian Steward (1955), Elman Service (1962), Morton Fried (1967), and Robert Carneiro (1970). This is the evolution of successively higher levels of sociopolitical integration—the appearance of new plateaus of human culture, qualitatively different structures when contrasted with earlier or simpler forms. The work of these men aroused several academic generations of anthropologists and wrought major improvements in archaeological interpretation until it bogged down, seemingly, in a series of near-fatal quibbles over terminology. Suddenly Service's "band, tribe, chiefdom, and state" became Fried's "egalitarian society, ranked society, and stratified society"; next the validity of "tribe" was being questioned, and eventually "chiefdom" was a dirty word. A heuristic framework of considerable utility had seemingly become a series of pigeonholes without which certain archaeologists seemed helpless, and into which other archaeologists were reluctant to force their data. One of the reluctant majority concluded in an overview, "I cannot see that this has gotten us very far in New World archaeology" (Coe 1977:25).

I am not as discouraged by this impasse as my colleagues, since I feel it can be circumvented by concentrating on the gradual appearance of specific sociopolitical institutions in the evolutionary record rather than on the problem of whether a given society is a tribe or a chiefdom. I will not pursue the point here, however, since it is not the emphasis of this chapter. One point of this chapter is that the fascina-

1

tion with general evolution that characterized the period from 1955 to 1975 caused many of us to ignore all other aspects of evolution. We were so concerned with the emergence of higher levels of integration that divergence, the "other kind of evolution," became an all-but-forgotten process.

DIVERGENCE, SPECIATION, AND ADAPTIVE RADIATION

The concept of adaptive radiation is at least as old as Darwin, and the classic example from biological evolution involves the finches of the Galápagos Islands (Lack 1947). Arriving in the Galápagos during the voyage of the *Beagle*, Darwin noted 14 closely related species of finches (*Geospiza* spp.) occupying different islands. He reasoned that a single ancestral species had reached the Galápagos from the South American mainland, and by island-hopping its members had eventually reached all parts of the archipelago. Now partially isolated from each other, the finches had adapted to local environmental conditions as well as undergoing non-adaptive divergence or drift, until they were different at the species level. This speciation had been accomplished without the appearance of any new life forms in the general evolutionary sense.

There is another observation that could be made about Darwin's finches, however, which is equally germane to the theoretical framework of this book. Each of those island species shares certain characteristics, including the shape of the skull, with all other finches in the world. This is the legacy of a more remote period, when finches split off from other perching birds. Each shares with other birds a series of characters, including feathers, that are the legacy of a still more remote era. It shares still other characters, including the ability to lay eggs, with the reptilian ancestors from which birds evolved. And so it goes, backward through time, to the evolution of the vertebrate skeleton, the segmented body, and bilateral symmetry. Every organism represents a complex combination of characters that are legacies from different stages in its evolutionary past, and only a few of which can be explained on the basis of its current adaptation.

Divergence from a common ancestor is one of the fundamental aspects of biological evolution, and it has undoubtedly played a major role in the evolution of the bewildering variety of human cultures with which the anthropologist is confronted. Each of those cultures also has a complex series of legacies from its evolutionary past, perhaps reinterpreted and integrated with adaptive innovations. Fortunately, even at the height of general evolutionism (between 1955 and 1975), a handful of anthropologists thought to focus their field and library research on this otherwise forgotten process. In this topic I will briefly review the approaches of Goodenough (1955) and Sahlins (1958) in Polynesia, Kot-

tak (1972) in Madagascar, Linares (1977) in Panama, the University of Chicago in highland Chiapas (McQuown and Pitt-Rivers 1970), and Lathrap (1976) on adaptive radiation in general. In Topic 2, Marcus reviews the "genetic model" of Romney (1957) and Vogt (1963, 1964).

In 1955, Goodenough proposed a reconstruction of the archaic form of Malayo–Polynesian kinship and descent, the generalized ancestral culture from which today's "daughter cultures" had sprung. He also considered the formal changes in kinship and descent that should have accompanied the divergence of these daughter systems. The principle used by Goodenough—reconstruction of an ancestral form from the common elements shared by its descendants—has been used by paleontologists, by archaeologists, and by linguists seeking to reconstruct a protolanguage.

That same year, Sahlins submitted a thesis (published in 1958) attempting to explain the divergence of Polynesian island societies from a common Proto-Polynesian ancestor. Sahlins's task was to explain the varieties of social ranking in Polynesia in terms of both adaptive radiation and nonadaptive divergence.

> The Polynesian cultures derive from a common source; they are members of a single cultural genus that has filled in and adapted to a variety of local habitats. Since the environments and the techniques of adaptation vary, it can be expected that the social systems correspondingly vary. . . .
> A word of warning. Our explanation of variation in terms of adaptation does not mean that such historical processes as diffusion are ignored. . . . The actual process of adaptation depends, to a great extent, on the previous cultural form and the outside influences upon it. One cannot have a complete understanding of the differences between two cultures without knowledge of their previous forms as well as of their present adaptations [Sahlins 1958:ix–x].

In 1956, within a year of the Goodenough and Sahlins papers, Lathrap independently produced a paper which made many of the same points but was not to be published for 20 years (Lathrap 1976:494). This paper was set in a hypothetical continent rather than an island system, and its relevance to the peopling of the New World should be immediately obvious.

> Let us picture an hypothetical continent extending through a wide range of latitudes and exhibiting a wide range of life zones. Let us introduce onto this continent at any point a small society with a subsistence pattern which is somewhat generalized. . . . The first thing which would be expectable is that the society should radiate and gradually send offshoot societies into all geographical areas of the continent which can be effectively utilized by the subsistence pattern of the original society. . . .
> After a long period of time the hypothetical continent should be almost completely occupied. Each society should be well adapted to its own immediate geographical environment. All of the societies should share a number of cultural elements due to the fact that all had diverged from a single cultural tradition, but in the course of time the shared cultural content should become progressively less due to cultural drift. The subsistence economies, although originally all of one pattern should show progressively greater divergence as each become more completely adapted to its own limited environment [Lathrap 1976:498–499].

While Lathrap was writing this paper, the University of Chicago was initiating a program of anthropological research in the highlands of Chiapas, Mexico, which was based on many of the same assumptions. Begun in 1956 and continuing through 1961, the Man in Nature Project (McQuown and Pitt-Rivers 1970) was originally designed to compare and contrast the Tzeltal and Tzotzil Maya from both synchronic and diachronic viewpoints. Glottochronological data had suggested that Tzeltal and Tzotzil were offshoots of a common ancestral language spoken 1300 years ago (Kaufman 1976:111). Since the Late Classic period in the Maya Highlands, the Tzeltal and Tzotzil had been diverging physically, culturally, and linguistically. The task of the Man in Nature Project was to analyze the Tzeltal and Tzotzil in terms of their common heritage, differing environmental adaptations, cultural and linguistic drift, and influence on each other. While scores of fascinating individual papers have resulted, the final synthesis explaining Tzeltal and Tzotzil diversity has yet to be written.

The Chiapas Project was, however, not the last effort to understand the adaptive radiation of two closely related American Indian groups. To the south, in Panama, Olga Linares analyzed "the evidence for divergence from a common origin with dispersal and colonization of two areas" by "two allotropic types of tropical forest agriculturalists, with distinct subsistence and settlement patterns" (Linares 1977:304). Linares chose as her research area two adjacent provinces which lead down to the coasts from Panama's Continental Divide. Bocas del Toro, flanking the Caribbean coast, has a mature tropical rain forest produced by 3500 mm of annual rainfall with no pronounced dry season. Chiriquí, on the Pacific coast, receives only 1800–2200 mm and has a pronounced dry season. The oldest ceramics found in both provinces (A.D. 300–600) are so similar as to suggest a common origin for the associated colonists, probably early speakers of Guaymí. However,

> in the process of migration and adaptation, each of these groups developed contrasting adaptations in accordance with existing differences in the geography and ecology of Bocas versus Chiriquí; vegeculture [root crop cultivation], the agricultural system developed by the Bocas groups, encouraged population displacement, small group-size and outside reliance on hunting and fishing; seed-culture [maize farming], as adopted by the Chiriquí Guaymí, permitted intensification, independence from other protein sources and a greater degree of sociopolitical elaboration [Linares 1977:315].

While Linares's model is primarily one of adaptive radiation into contrasting environments, she does not forget nonadaptive divergence, nor does she ignore the specific legacy of the common ancestral culture: "If processes of culture change are to be gauged, evaluated or even described, the initial state of the culture must be known. This seems obvious, but it is often ignored by archaeologists" (Linares 1977:313). This point is already made in the extended quotation from Sahlins, who goes on to point out that "one could not explain the biological differences between primates and earthworms simply from the fact that primates

took to the trees whereas earthworms took to the earth" (Sahlins 1958:x). Each culture is a product not merely of its current adaptation but of its past history.

Kottak's model for adaptive radiation on the island of Madagascar is one of the most complex, for it involves not only specific evolution (divergence from a common ancestor) but general evolution as well (the appearance of new levels of sociopolitical integration). According to Kottak (1972 and personal communication), the Proto-Malagasy arrived on the island around A.D. 1 speaking a Malayo-Polynesian language related to that of the Barito of Borneo, who are inland horticulturalists. Their East African phenotype is explained by the theory that they had colonized the East African coast as maritime traders before reaching Madagascar. Many Malagasy structural traits—their kinship, social organization, foster parentage systems, divination rituals, and certain religious concepts—appear throughout the island and demonstrate a common origin.

From a probable entry point on the north coast, populations spread down the east and west coasts, with linguistic divergence becoming significant by the seventh century A.D. By A.D. 1300, migrants from the east coast had penetrated the interior, bringing wet rice into an area where it could be intensively irrigated. The Malagasy eventually radiated into at least six major "adaptive types," each composed of several ethnic groups. These included river valley agriculturalists like the Taisaka, swidden cultivators like the Tanala, and pastoralists like the Bara. By A.D. 1800, the Merina—irrigated rice farmers of the interior—had achieved the level of a state, with kings who unified and dominated the surrounding population. Madagascar offers such potential as a laboratory for the study of adaptive radiation and cultural evolution that Henry Wright has recently begun an archaeological investigation of the Merina region (Wright and Kus 1979).

The Madagascar data contribute two more processes relevant to the model developed in this volume: *parallel* and *convergent* evolution. Where two neighboring populations are in continuous contact, as were some of the Malagasy societies, innovations may be exchanged with such regularity that a kind of parallel evolution takes place over a period of time. Alternatively, after a long separation, two societies may converge either as the result of a similar adaptation or of the acculturative effects of a third society. In the case of Madagascar, French colonial rule between 1896 and 1960 imposed a kind of pan-Malagasy uniformity over previously divergent societies. In the case of the Mesoamerican Indians discussed in this book, there were moments of convergence effected by Toltec imperialism, Aztec conquest, and 500 years of colonial Spanish rule.

ARCHAEOLOGY AND SPECIFIC EVOLUTION

By now the major argument of this topic should be clear. While the "neoevolutionists" of the period 1955 to 1975 were aware of the relationship between general and specific evolution, most of them were far more interested in general evolution. The major books and articles of that period usually dealt with "progress," with man's "ascent" from hunting and gathering to urban civilization.[1] Ethnologists made a much-appreciated contribution to our understanding of general evolution until they became bogged down in an argument over how many levels of progress there were, and what they should be called.

[1]And general evolution has remained the major concern of most archaeological articles which have appeared since this book went to press (see, for example, Yoffee 1979, Dunnell 1980).

Only in a few cases, such as those mentioned above, did ethnologists attempt to trace the specific evolutionary history of societies diverging from a common ancestor. After all, some of the societies were preliterate, and some of the processes stretched over hundreds or even thousands of years. Here was a challenge for the archaeologist. Yet instead of accepting the challenge, we archaeologists of that period mostly stood around, pencil in hand, writing down the characteristics of tribes and chiefdoms as the ethnologists dictated them. Perhaps their current terminological impasse will enable us to get back to the other aspects of evolution, which have lain fallow for so long.

TOPIC 2
The Genetic Model and the Linguistic Divergence of the Otomangueans

JOYCE MARCUS

Topic 1 has been devoted to some general aspects of divergent evolution. In Topic 2, we will focus more specifically on the divergent evolution of the Zapotec and Mixtec people, who are the subject of this volume. We will begin with the generally accepted position that the Zapotec and Mixtec languages, both tonal, had a common ancestry far back in time, and we will present a tentative chronology for their subsequent linguistic divergence. Next we will discuss a framework known as the *genetic model*, which has previously been used to organize data on the divergent evolution of Maya-speaking peoples. This will lead us to a brief outline of the approach used in this volume.

Most classifications of Mesoamerican Indians have relied on linguistic relatedness or affinity as one of their organizing principles, and according to these criteria the Zapotec and Mixtec belong to the Otomanguean family (Fernández de Miranda, Swadesh, and Weitlaner 1960; Swadesh 1967). This large language family, perhaps the "oldest" in Mesoamerica in terms of time depth in the area, is sometimes described as including the following language groups:

I. Zapotecan	IV. Chinantecan
1. Zapotec	1. Chinantec
2. Chatino	V. Popolocan
II. Mixtecan	1. Popoloca
1. Mixtec	2. Ixcatec
2. Cuicatec	3. Chocho
3. Trique	4. Mazatec
III. Otopamean	VI. Huave
1. Pame	VII. Amuzgo
2. Chichimeca-Jonaz	VIII. Manguean
3. Otomí	1. Chiapanec
4. Mazahua	2. Mangue
5. Matlatzinca	3. Diria
6. Ocuilteca	4. Cholutec

5. Nicoya	7. Nagrandan
6. Orisi	8. Orotinya

It should be noted that there is no universal agreement on this classification, which emerged from a conference held in 1957 covering glottochronology and the Otomanguean languages. Swadesh at one point wanted to exclude category VIII, the Manguean group, because all these languages are now extinct; he also felt that their relationship to categories I–VII was tenuous (Longacre 1967). One suggestion was to rename groups I–VII *Macro-Mixtecan* because of the "centrality" of Mixtec to the whole network of languages (Fernández de Miranda, Swadesh, and Weitlaner 1960); another suggestion was to create a category called *Oaxacan* which would include groups I, II, V, and VII (Swadesh 1967). In spite of these disagreements, the term *Otomanguean* has remained in common usage, even in contexts where groups I–VII are discussed. The reconstructed ancestral language from which all these recent tongues descended has usually been referred to as *Proto–Otomanguean*.

We should make it clear from the outset that this volume will not mention group VIII, the extinct Manguean languages of Chiapas and Central America. We are primarily concerned with groups I (Zapotec, Chatino) and II (Mixtec, Cuicatec, and Trique), although from time to time it will be necessary for us to mention groups III, IV, and V. We must do so because our discussions of Preceramic Oaxaca take us back to a time before any of these languages had diverged from each other (Chapter 2).

We will use the term *Otomanguean* in this volume because it is in common usage in the anthropological literature, and because we do not feel that we, as archaeologists, should propose yet another term when linguists cannot even agree on the terms we already have. Nevertheless, it should be understood that our comments really apply only to languages spoken from the present state of Hidalgo in the north to Oaxaca in the south.

GLOTTOCHRONOLOGY

Just as linguists are not in total agreement as to whether Macro-Mixtecan or Otomanguean is the best inclusive category for the related tonal languages of Oaxaca, they are not in total agreement about the order in which these various languages split off from each other. In this volume, we have chosen to follow the scheme set forth by Fernández de Miranda, Swadesh, and Weitlaner (1960), since in that paper the authors attempted to resolve some of the disagreements existing at the time of the 1957 conference on glottochronology.

At the present time, glottochronology, a part of lexicostatistics, is the only technique providing some measure of time depth that might be useful to archaeologists. It is a technique of linguistic comparison based on the following principles:

1. When different languages have certain kinds of similarities that must stem from a similar earlier language, the people speaking them must also once have formed a single community, or have had very long and direct contact with descendants of that community.

2. Since degrees of similarity among these languages imply recency of separation or of continued contact after separation, general inferences can be made that bear on the time and location for prehistoric contact and unity.

3. Cognate words discovered during the process of demonstrating the common origin of two or more languages provide us with evidence for shared cultural traits or features of the physical environment they shared.

4. Other words not having cognates among the languages (especially if identifiable as loan words from a specific source) may provide us with evidence for contacts with other groups in prehistory (Swadesh 1967:79).

Thus, although in general terms language change is slow and gradual and follows specific patterns of change, the lexicostatistic method of language classification takes into account the fact that language affinity and similarity depend not only on how recently two languages were separated, but also on the degree and amount of contact maintained during the period of separation and differentiation. As Swadesh (1967:80) points out, linguistic communities tend to develop regional variants and greater similarity can be seen between neighboring dialects, while less similarity is seen when the geographic distance is increased or the degree of social interaction is reduced.

Obviously, if any form of linguistic classification is to complement and help in the reconstruction of prehistory, it is crucial that we have some information on the time depth of the divergences. As we have seen, "time depth" in this instance is not a simple measure of time, because it must reflect both degree and duration of separation. This problem has been resolved by linguists by determining what they call "minimum time depth." Therefore, in a set of related languages within which minimum time depth between each set of two languages can be established, we know that the group as a whole has a time depth equal to (or greater than) that of the largest minimum separation found in the group. To determine maximum time depth of divergence, we need to compare the languages within this group to others that are more distantly related. After following these procedures and obtaining both minimum and maximum time depth divergences, we can then attempt to relate the divergent evolution of languages to the archaeological record in various geographical regions, as Beals (1969) has done.

Glottochronological information must be used with caution. In 1960, Dell Hymes stated:

> It is tempting to think of reasons why glottochronology should not work, and some find it hard to accept the fact that it can. It is tempting for an anthropologist to use even provisional findings of linguistic relationship and time depth, and some find it hard not to accept them uncritically. Either may be unfortunate. Extreme skepticism delays the maturity of glottochronology, and of lexicostatistics, the field of which it is so far a part. Rash use of provisional results may give way to rash disillusionment [1960:3].

What separates glottochronology from other comparative linguistic classifications is quantification. From the nineteenth century on, scholars had recognized that the amount of linguistic change had to be related to, or was a function of, time (Schmidt 1872; Schuchardt 1900; Sapir 1916). Initially, ethnographers had counted up the number of cognate words to determine whether two languages were closely related or not. An advance over this method was made by Sapir (1916), who assessed the amount of divergence in phonetic and structural aspects of New World languages by comparing them with historically known languages in Europe and the Old World. In other words, he used the Indo-European languages (and especially the Germanic and Romance groups) as his "control" for determining scales of time depth and quantification.

As is well known to archaeologists, radiocarbon dating proved to be encouraging and fairly reliable when it was introduced in the late 1940s by Libby. What is less well known is that this breakthrough in dating was one of the factors that encouraged Swadesh to seek a comparable technique in linguistics. Swadesh felt that the vocabulary of a language could be made to yield the percentage of words that resist change after separation or divergence. Accordingly, he composed a diagnostic word list and, like Sapir, compared it to historically known languages; he found some agreement in retention rates of words (Swadesh 1951). The average retention rates in all the test cases were taken as the index for determining minimum time of separation. Therefore, the typical application to prehistory consists of comparing the diagnostic "basic vocabulary" lists of two languages that are supposed to have common ancestry. At the present time glottochronology, although needing greater refinement just as our other dating methods do, can be a very useful tool for archaeologists.

STAGES IN THE DIVERGENCE OF OTOMANGUEAN

Ralph Beals (1969) was one of the first to attempt to combine archaeological data with the timetable provided by linguists for the divergence of the Otomanguean languages. Even more archaeological data are now available for such an attempt, however, than Beals had at his disposal. A review of the glottochronological evidence reveals discrete periods of great activity (during which many languages split off from each other) and long periods of stability (in which few separations took place). It is possible that this feature is an artifact of the glottochronological method. Alternatively, it is possible that these discrete "stages" or "periods" reflect economic, social, or political events that sped up or slowed down the physical separation of linguistic groups. An approach similar to Beals's might suggest the following stages in the divergent evolution of Otomanguean language groups I–VII.

Stage 1, circa 10,000 B.C. At this stage in the region known as Mesoamerica, there may have been only one language spoken, ancestral to all of the languages of the Otomanguean, Mayan, and Utoaztecan peoples today (Swadesh 1967:87–89, Figs. 1, 2). Archaeologically, this stage falls within the Paleoindian period, and so little is known of this period that we cannot even state definitively whether the various regions of Mesoamerica appear culturally homogeneous or heterogeneous.

Stage 2, 8000–5000 B.C. Sometime during this period, an ancestral language called Proto-Otomanguean must have diverged from its now-distant Mayan and Utoaztecan relatives. Since that language was ancestral to Zapotec, Chatino, Mixtec, Trique, Amuzgo, Cuicatec, Chinantec, Mazatec, Chocho, Popoloca, and Otomí, we suggest in Chapter 2 that it may have been the language of the Preceramic hunters and gatherers of what are today the highlands of Hidalgo, Toluca, Tlaxcala, Puebla, and Oaxaca. Beals (1969:322) has expressed a similar view, and we differ from him mainly by our inclusion of the Isthmus of Tehuantepec in the Mixe–Zoque region, rather than in the Otomanguean area, at this early period. Considering the languages that have since arisen from Proto-Otomanguean, it was possibly already a tonal language.

Stage 3, roughly 5100–4100 B.C. During this period a number of divergences occurred among language groups which Fernández de Miranda, Swadesh, and Weitlaner (1960:146–149) describe as having "remote relationships." The Otomí–Pame group split off from the Mixtec–Zapotec group between 4800 and 4100 B.C. (68 minimum centuries separate Otomí from Trique). The Chinantec also split off

from the Mixtec–Zapotec group during this period (71 minimum centuries separate Chinantec from Amuzgo; 68 separate Chinantec from Zapotec). The Proto-Otomí speakers to the north may have adjoined the Proto–Mixtec speakers, and are thought by some to have been centered in the Valley of Toluca (Carrasco 1950; Wolf 1959). The present-day Chinantecs live in the eastern mountains of Oaxaca, north of the Zapotec and east and southeast of the Mazatec; Beals (1969) suggests that the Proto-Chinantecans may have moved southward to their present location.

Archaeologically, the Chinantla went on to diverge from the rest of the Otomanguean area, with Formative affinities to the Gulf Coast lowlands of Mexico; the Otomí area went on to show affinities with the Valley of Mexico.

Stage 4, roughly 4100–3700 B.C. This stage was a period of linguistic change. The Chocho–Popoloca–Mazatec group split off from Mixtecan, a divergence that might be reflected archaeologically in differences between the Tehuacán Valley and the Ñuiñe area on the one hand and the Mixteca on the other. Since Mixtec and Chatino are separated by 57 minimum centuries (Fernández de Miranda, Swadesh, and Weitlaner 1960:148), I conclude that the Mixtec–Cuicatec stem and the Zapotec–Chatino stem had begun to diverge by 3700 B.C. This important event, the initial separation of the ancestors of the Mixtec and Zapotec, took place during a period of Preceramic hunting, gathering, and slowly evolving agriculture.

Stage 5, roughly 2100–1300 B.C. This was also a period of abundant linguistic change. Here we move from language groups with "remote" relationships to groups of only "distant" relationships, in the terms of Fernández de Miranda, Swadesh, and Weitlaner (1960:145–146). Cuicatec split off from Mixtec of the Cuyamecalco region by 1300 B.C. (33 minimum centuries) and is believed to have moved south. Amuzgo split off from Mixtec of the same region by 1700 B.C. (37 minimum centuries), and is also thought to have moved south (Fernández de Miranda, Swadesh, and Weitlaner 1960:145–146). Trique split off from the Costa Chica dialect of Mixtec by 2100 B.C. (41 minimum centuries), but it is not known archaeologically when the Mixtecs actually reached the Costa Chica. To the south, the neighboring Mixe and Zoque had begun their linguistic divergence by 1500 B.C. (35 minimum centuries). It is probable that many of these linguistic separations are somehow related to the increasing population and regional adaptation that accompanied sedentary agriculture.

Longacre and Millon (1961) have attempted to reconstruct Proto-Mixtecan, the language ancestral to Mixtec, Cuicatec, Chocho–Popoloca, Mazatec, Amuzgo, and Trique, which would have been spoken at the time these Stage 5 separations began. According to their reconstruction, Proto-Mixtecan would have included such words as *cacao, maguey, maguey fiber, maize, avocado, chile, beans, amaranth, metate, to spin* and *to weave*. They list other words as "probably present"—*pine torch, squash, tobacco, tumpline, village, pulque,* and *zapote.* They further suggest that the Proto-Mixtecans employed a simple form of the vigesimal system, and that their world may have been populated by "deities" related to natural phenomena. While some of these suggestions (e.g., *pulque, cacao,* and *tobacco*) have not as yet been archaeologically demonstrated for this period in Oaxaca, many of the others have been (see Byers 1967).

Stage 6, 400 B.C.–A.D. 100. This stage is the period of languages with "recent relations," in the terms of Fernández de Miranda, Swadesh, and Weitlaner (1960:140–145). Between 400 and 300 B.C. (23–24 minimum centuries), Mazatec separated from Chocho–Popoloca. And at roughly A.D. 100 (18–20 minimum centuries), Chatino began to separate from Zapotec; this separation may correspond to a Chatino movement toward the Pacific Coast.

Stage 7, A.D. 500–1000. During this period, there were internal divergences within Zapotec, with the Miahuatlán dialect and Sierra dialect separating from that of the Valley of Oaxaca. This divergence might reflect lessened contact among the valley, the Sierra, and the Miahuatlán area following the decline of Monte Albán (Chapter 7).

Stage 8, circa A.D. 1200–1400. Chocho separated from Popoloca (8 minimum centuries) and Isthmus Zapotec separated from Valley Zapotec (6–8 minimum centuries). While the latter is presumed to reflect the Postclassic Zapotec expansion to the Isthmus of Tehuantepec, displacing the Huave and perhaps the Mixe as well, archaeological data suggest the Zapotec had been there many centuries earlier (Chapter 8). This suggestion, in turn, underscores the glottochronologists' reasons for insisting that their dates are only in "minimum" centuries for separation.

GLOTTOCHRONOLOGY AND RADIOCARBON DATES

There is a problem in the correlation of archaeological and glottochronological data that has generally not been discussed by the authors who have attempted it. Linguistic divergence is given by glottochronologists in minimum centuries before the present, the scale being what is sometimes referred to as "real" time. Archaeologists give their dates in radiocarbon years before the present; we now know that these differ from real time because one of the original basic assumptions of radiocarbon dating—that the amount of $^{14}CO_2$ in the atmosphere has remained constant—has been found to be incorrect (Olsson 1970; Suess 1970).

Over the last decade, various workers have attempted to chart the fluctuations of atmospheric radiocarbon and to establish the relationship between radiocarbon dates and real time by radiocarbon-dating the growth rings of long-lived trees (such as the sequoia and bristlecone pine) whose ages in real years have been established by dendrochronology. A recent synthesis of the results (Ralph, Michael, and Han 1973) shows that for some ancient periods, such as 5000–4000 B.C., there may be as much as 800 or 900 years difference between real time and radiocarbon time. This

TABLE 1.1

Approximate Correspondence between Radiocarbon Dates and "Real" Time As Determined by Dendrochronology[a]

^{14}C dates (5568-year half-life)	Dendrochronology dates
A.D. 1500	A.D. 1420
A.D. 1000	A.D. 1020
A.D. 500	A.D. 546
0	A.D. 50
500 B.C.	660–730 B.C.
1000 B.C.	1240–1270 B.C.
1500 B.C.	1800 B.C.
2000 B.C.	2560 B.C.
2500 B.C.	3190–3310 B.C.
3000 B.C.	3760 B.C.
3500 B.C.	4380 B.C.
4000 B.C.	4910 B.C.
4500 B.C.	5320 B.C.

[a]After Ralph, Michael, and Han (1973).

would amount to 8 or 9 minimum centuries in glottochronological terms, a considerable margin for error.

In this volume, all radiocarbon dates will be given as recommended by the journal *Radiocarbon:* they will be calculated using the "old" 5568-year half-life for ^{14}C and subtracting the B.P. date from 1950. This is the procedure followed by Drennan in the Appendix, which lists all known radiocarbon dates from Oaxaca. We will not convert our dates to the "new" 5730-year half-life because, in our opinion, this practice has already introduced considerable confusion into the archaeological record. In some cases, it has been used by recent excavators to make their sites appear somewhat "older" than coeval sites that were excavated before the new half-life was discovered.

In comparing linguistic divergences with archaeological time periods, we will attempt to correlate the two by using the extensive table given by Ralph, Michael, and Han (1973), which compares tree-ring and radiocarbon chronologies.[1] An outline of this correlation may be found in Table 1.1.

As an example of how this correspondence works, let us consider the initial separation of the Cloud People, the period in which Zapotecan (Zapotec and Chatino) split off from Mixtecan (Mixtec, Cuicatec, Trique). We have already seen that this process is believed to have taken place 57 minimum centuries ago, or about 3700 B.C. in "real" time (Fernández de Miranda, Swadesh, and Weitlaner 1960:148). However, 3700 B.C. in real time corresponds to 3000 B.C. in radiocarbon years (5568-year half-life), a date that falls in the Blanca phase in the Valley of Oaxaca and the Abejas phase in the Valley of Tehuacán. This finding directs us to search in the archaeological data from those phases for independent evidence for the gradual separation of Mixtecan and

---

[1]Ralph, Michael, and Han use the 5730-year half-life. We have converted their dates to the 5568-year half-life in order to conform to the policy followed by *Radiocarbon.*

Zapotecan peoples. Had we failed to make the adjustment of time scales and assumed a date of 3700 B.C. in radiocarbon years, two completely different archaeological phases would be involved.

Obviously, it would be foolish to seek precision too fine in either time scale; they are only guidelines, figures which are probably in the right ballpark without necessarily being in the right box seat. Future glottochronological studies may well modify our estimates in minimum centuries, and we can expect continuing readjustments in radiocarbon chronology. All we have done in this volume is make as close an approximation as possible in October 1975.

THE GENETIC MODEL

While linguists were engaged in working out the divergent evolution of Mesoamerican languages through glottochronology, ethnologists were considering the possibility of a related, but even more complex, phenomenon: the physical and cultural divergence of the Indians who spoke those languages. Researchers such as Eggan (1954), Romney (1957), and Vogt (1963, 1964) began experimenting with a framework called "the genetic model."

> The genetic model takes as its segment of cultural history a group of tribes which are set off from all other groups by sharing a common physical type, possessing common systemic patterns, and speaking genetically related languages. It is assumed that correspondence among these three factors indicates a common historical tradition at some time in the past for these tribes. We shall designate this segment of cultural history as the "genetic unit" and it includes the ancestral group and all intermediate groups, as well as the tribes in the ethnographic present. The genetic unit represents a substantive segment of cultural history while the term "genetic model" refers to the conceptual framework which serves as a tool to order the data [Romney 1957:36].

In some ways the term *genetic model* was an unfortunate choice, for it conjures up a biological image that is misleading: cultural and linguistic divergence play as large a role as (if not larger than) biological divergence in all the examples these authors have given us. As discussed by Vogt (1964:11–12), the application of the genetic model involves the combined use of a number of linguistic, archaeological, physical anthropological, ethnological, and historical methods. He views the genetic model, when applied to human populations, as dealing with how a small protogroup succeeds in adapting to a certain ecological niche and developing certain patterns that would constitute the basic protoculture; further, if the adaptation is successful, the group may begin to split and radiate from a point of dispersal that has sometimes been called the homeland.

Perhaps the most comprehensive attempt to apply the genetic model can be seen in the symposium volume *Desarrollo Cultural de los Mayas,* edited by Vogt and Ruz Lhuillier (1964). The theme and substance of the volume have been admirably summarized by a reviewer who is himself interested in evolution:

The unifying theme throughout the collection is that of the genetic model and its application to Maya anthropology. The main elements of the concept may be summarized as follows:

1. Tribes or ethnic groups that share a common physical type, systemic patterns, and genetically related languages may be grouped together as a unit of historical analysis. The similarities are ascribed to common origins at some time in the past.

2. The various groups all descended from a relatively small group that resided in a restricted geographical area. Through migrations descendants of this original group spread over an extensive territory, and the original unit became internally differentiated in all three characteristics (i.e., physical type, language, systemic patterns). The argument here is that as one traces the history of each group backward in time, there is convergence.

3. It is recognized that as the group differentiated, adaptation to diverse environments, unselected drift, and contact with foreign groups caused these divergences from the original proto-culture.

4. Methodologically speaking, the basis of defining such genetic units should be linguistic because of the relative exactness of linguistic methods as compared to those of ethnography and archaeology.

5. The method of defining such units would consist of the following steps: plotting the distribution of the related languages, calculating the approximate time depth of the linguistic differentiation, defining the area of origin and the history of migrations, reconstructing the proto-language and proto-culture from linguistic data, testing the reconstruction by archaeological data, testing the reconstruction by physical anthropological data, and, finally, analyzing systemic patterns in existence today.

By applying the above methodology, a series of problems of Maya culture history was attacked: (1) origin of the Maya linguistically, racially, and culturally; (2) origin of the basic elements of Lowland Maya civilization, such as the pyramid temple, calendar, religious symbols, subsistence; (3) identification of the Petén Maya as to linguistic affiliation; (4) overall relationships between the Lowland Maya and outside groups such as the Highland Maya and non-Maya, and the role of such groups in the history of Lowland Maya civilization; (5) problem of the decline of the Petén Maya; (6) problem of the socioeconomic integration of the Classic Maya; and (7) origin of the specific characteristics of Lowland Maya civilization [Sanders 1966:1069; reproduced by permission of the American Anthropological Association, *American Anthropologist* 68(5):1068–1071, 1966].

While describing this work as "perhaps the most successful attempt in New World anthropology" to "interrelate ethnographic, linguistic, and archaeological data," Sanders also has a number of criticisms to offer. He finds the idea of a cultural tradition (systemic pattern) persisting through 4000 years and over an area of nearly 300,000 km² "improbable." He clearly feels that environmental factors should be more heavily emphasized in explaining the divergence of various Maya groups. He also questions the utility of knowing that certain institutions, such as the patrilineage, had great temporal and spatial tenacity, pointing out that such institutions "may well preserve their basic structure, yet have completely different functions as they became adapted to new situations" (Sanders 1966:1070).

Since we use a similar model of divergent evolution in this volume, we should respond to these criticisms. First of all, we do not find it at all surprising that certain basic cultural patterns should persist over a large area for 4000 years; in fact, we find it likely that certain patterns displayed by the Zapotec and Mixtec persisted for more than 8000 years. The key lies in the very concept of "becoming adapted to new situations" that Sanders has expressed. The pattern that survives is precisely the one with sufficient inherent flexibility to be continuously readapted to changes in both "general" and "specific" evolution. The radius and ulna did not disappear when birds achieved their general evolutionary ascent from reptiles; they became the bones of the wing. Nor did they vanish when penguins achieved their specific evolutionary divergence from other birds; they became the bones of the flipper. In evolutionary terms, it is just as important to know the homologies of the reptile forelimb, the penguin's flipper, and the eagle's wing as it is to know that they are respectively adapted to land, water, and air.

Had we enough data we might, in a similar way, be able to trace the concept of the four world quarters, each with its primary color, through from the Proto-Otomangueans to the Postclassic Indians of Southern Mexico (see Topic 9). On a Formative level it appears to have served as a way of organizing the barrios of a large Oaxacan village (Pyne 1976:280); on a later and more complex level, it may help explain why Classic Zapotec mound groups so often consisted of four pyramids on the north, south, east, and west sides of a patio. On a much larger regional level, I have already pointed to a hieroglyphic inscription in stone which suggests that the lowland Maya of A.D. 731 conceived of four major centers—Tikal, Calakmul (?), Palenque, and Copán—associated with the four world quarters (Marcus 1976a:Fig. 1.9). And as late as the 1950s the concept helped explain a color–direction ritual in acculturated Zapotec Oaxaca (Weitlaner and de Cicco 1962; Marcus and Flannery 1978). The way in which such organizing principles are readapted at successively higher levels of sociopolitical integration is one fascinating aspect of evolution, and helps explain why these principles do survive for 4000 years or more.

THE OUTLINE OF THIS VOLUME

In the course of this volume, we hope to trace through time both the divergent evolution of the Zapotec and Mixtec from a common ancestral culture and their general evolution through successively higher levels of sociopolitical evolution. In doing this, the various authors will employ glot-

tochronological evidence, archaeological evidence, and ethnohistoric evidence for both types of evolution.

We fully realize that not all readers will feel comfortable with our version of the genetic model. For this reason, we have used it primarily as a framework for organizing our data on the Zapotec and Mixtec, rather than as a universal model for which we must act as advocates. We have tried to include enough raw data in this volume to offer something even to those readers who lack interest in the model. Those who are interested in the model will almost certainly think of ways in which it could be applied to their own data.

As the Cloud People diverged from a common ancestor, they, like the Maya studied by Vogt and Ruz Lhuillier, underwent changes of three kinds. They adapted to diverse environments; they underwent unselected "drift"; and they were influenced by neighboring foreign cultures. At the same time, they retained a whole series of characteristics that set them apart from other Mesoamerican peoples and that continued to provide evidence for their common ancestry despite modification and readaptation. One challenge of Oaxacan archaeology is to understand how all those diverse processes produced the cultures we know as Zapotec and Mixtec.

Sanders's review of Vogt and Ruz Lhuillier makes it clear that many archaeologists will be disappointed with us unless we come up with an environmental explanation for virtually every difference between the Zapotec and Mixtec. Unfortunately, it cannot be done. Still other archaeologists will be disappointed if we attribute those differences to anything but the "mental systems" of the Indians involved. That cannot be done either. Environmental differences go a long way toward explaining why the Valley Zapotec practiced well irrigation while the Nochixtlán Mixtec constructed *lama-bordo* systems (Topic 94), but they do not go very far toward explaining why lightning was a more important supernatural for the Zapotec, or why the Mixtec had a separate vocabulary for the hereditary lord's anatomy.

Of course, one could say (and some will) that the last-mentioned characteristics are not important, that once you get past the variables which are most directly linked to the environment you have entered the sphere of epiphenomena. That viewpoint was once a fashionable form of reductionism. But increasingly over the last decade many American archaeologists—including the one to whom this book is dedicated—have decided that whether it is fashionable or not, they are still anthropologists, and still interested in the study of culture. This book is for them.

The Common Origin of the Mixtec and Zapotec

Editors' Introduction

Our story begins at a time when the ancestors of the Cloud People all spoke one common language. The archaeological period involved was the era of seminomadic hunting, gathering, and incipient agriculture that preceded the manufacture of ceramics and the establishment of village life in Mesoamerica. The general region involved is assumed to have been the central and southern Mexican highlands (Figure 2.1), an area which at the time of the conquest was occupied by speakers of the Otomanguean language family. The environmental setting, so far as we have been able to reconstruct it, was one of forested mountains and valleys (see Topic 3). Here we are making the additional assumption, fairly well supported by the archaeological data, that the Otomanguean expansion to the Pacific Coast did not take place until after village life had been established.

Prior to 5000 B.C., the linguistic ancestors of the Zapotec, Mixtec, and Otomí all spoke one language—an ancestral tongue called Proto-Otomanguean (the glottochronological evidence is summarized in Topic 2). Precisely where the Proto-Otomanguean "heartland" lay has always been a subject of speculation, and in our opinion, it would be futile to try to specify it precisely. If 500 persons is the typical size of a "dialect tribe" (see Topic 8), given the low population density of Preceramic hunters and gatherers in the area we are discussing no valley would have had enough speakers for a dialect tribe. In fact, archaeological data suggest that there may have been times when there were barely 500 persons in the entire area comprising the Valley of Oaxaca, the Mixteca Alta, and the Tehuacán Valley. We would reconstruct the period as one of small, local bands of foragers who traveled enormous distances and were often forced to seek marriage partners from neighboring valleys. Therefore, rather than trying to single out one valley as the Otomanguean heartland, we would argue that the Proto-Otomangueans can be defined simply as the early Preceramic hunter–gatherers of the whole region from the state of Hidalgo (where the Otomí now live) to Puebla and Oaxaca (where the Mixtec and Zapotec now live). We would argue further that their low population density, which encouraged an extensive network of kinship and economic ties over a large area of the central and southern highlands, initially prevented the various valleys of the Proto-Otomanguean region from separating and drifting apart linguistically.

This period of early hunting and gathering included the Paleoindian cultures of the late Pleistocene, the El Riego phase of the Tehuacán Valley, and the Naquitz phase of the Valley of Oaxaca (see Topic 6). Toward the end of this period (about 5100–4800 B.C. in glottochronological terms), Chinantec and Otomí–Pame are thought to have begun their divergence from the Mixtec–Zapotec trunk. Mixtec–Zapotec, however, remained united through all of the Coxcatlán phase in the Tehuacán Valley and the Jícaras phase in the Valley of Oaxaca. Finally, between 4100 and 3700 B.C. in glottochronological terms (3500–3000 B.C. in radiocarbon years), the Zapotec–Chatino language group split off from the Mixtec–Cuicatec group. This was the initial separation of the Cloud People; during much of that same period, the Chocho–Popoloca–Mazatec language group began diverging from Mixtecan. This latter split should be reflected archaeologically in a divergence of the Tehuacán Valley from the Mixteca and the Valley of Oaxaca, a divergence which may be partially reflected in the

11

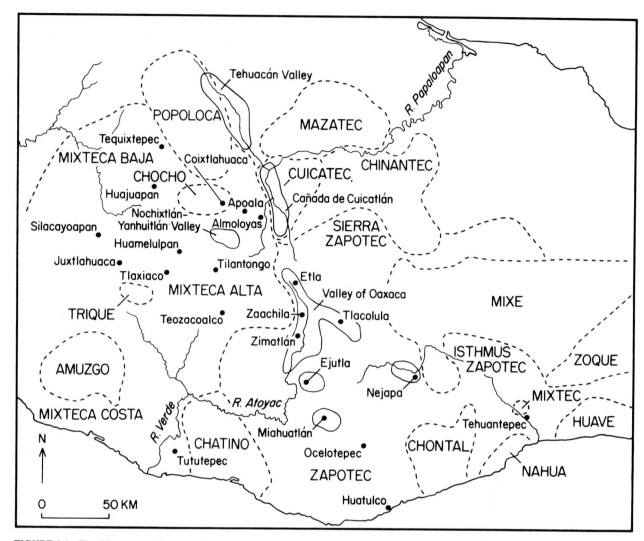

FIGURE 2.1. The Mixtec and Zapotec linguistic regions in southern Mexico, showing many of the localities mentioned in this volume. Major valley systems are delimited with a solid line, linguistic groups with a dashed line. Also shown are some neighboring language areas.

different frequencies of projectile point types between the Abejas phase in the Tehuacán Valley and the coeval Blanca phase in the Valley of Oaxaca (see Topic 6).

During the next 1500 years (3700–2100 B.C. in glottochronological terms, 3000–1500 B.C. in radiocarbon years), the Mixtec and the Zapotec should have drifted apart linguistically. This drift is not well documented archaeologically, however, because so little is known of the late Preceramic of the southern Mexican highlands (late Abejas phase in Tehuacán, Martínez phase in the Oaxaca region). Settlement patterns, material culture, and subsistence strategies appear to be similar in the Mixteca and the Valley of Oaxaca, in spite of the presumed linguistic divergence.

Agriculture increased in importance during this period, and village life was a reality everywhere in the area by 1500 B.C. (radiocarbon years). In our opinion, sedentary life probably accelerated the process of linguistic divergence in sever-

al ways. First, the move to village-based agriculture may have greatly reduced the mobility of each local group. Second, the population increases that accompanied sedentary life—resulting from the reduction of such factors as infant mortality and the time interval between births (see Binford and Chasko 1976)—soon produced "effective breeding populations" of 175 and dialect tribes of 500 persons within valley systems, making it unnecessary to procure mates from neighboring valleys. These increases probably made it easier for speakers of various dialects of Otomanguean to lose contact with one another.

In this chapter, several participants in the Santa Fe seminar present their current perspectives on Preceramic Oaxaca. Smith and Hopkins's paper (Topic 3) presents an outline of the range of environmental diversity in the Otomanguean region, a necessary prerequisite for any study of divergent evolution. Finally, in Topic 9 we deal with the cultural legacy of the Proto-Otomangueans. Using an approach which is similar to glottochronology, we have searched for similarities in the way the Mixtec and Zapotec classified the world—similarities so basic that they may go back to that ancient period before the Cloud People had separated.

TOPIC 3
Environmental Contrasts in the Otomanguean Region

C. EARLE SMITH, JR.
JOSEPH W. HOPKINS III

Editors' Note

Before we begin our reconstruction of the divergent evolution of the Zapotec and Mixtec out of a common ancestor, we should establish the natural setting in which that evolution occurred. Oaxaca is one of the most mountainous regions in all of Mexico, with variations in altitude and rainfall producing a wide variety of environments. The most densely settled areas are the flat, alluvial valleys of the major rivers in the area, although settlements also occur in canyons, in tributary valleys, on the piedmont, and in the higher mountains.

As a sample of the environmental variation in the region presently occupied by Otomanguean speakers, we will briefly consider four of the larger valleys in the area. The valleys of Oaxaca (Zapotec), Nochixtlán (Mixtec), and Tehuacán (Popoloca or Mazatec) are covered by C. Earle Smith, Jr. and the Cañada de Cuicatlán (Cuicatec) is covered by Joseph W. Hopkins III.

The Valleys of Oaxaca, Nochixtlán, and Tehuacán

C. EARLE SMITH, JR.

My discussion of these three valleys is drawn from a larger work on Precolumbian adaptations in Mexico (C. E. Smith n.d.).

THE VALLEY OF OAXACA

To the south of the Nochixtlán Valley lies the only broad riverine valley of southern Mexico. The wishbone-shaped Oaxaca Valley is drained by the Río Atoyac, running roughly from north to south. The base of the wishbone to the north is the Etla arm of the valley, while the higher Tlacolula arm to the southeast is drained by the Río Salado, tributary to the Atoyac. Finally, the other long arm of the wishbone, the Zaachila arm, is the lower course of the Río Atoyac and the broadest, lowest arm of the valley. The valley lies at an average elevation of 1550 m. Apparently, a resistant sill at the entrance to the Ayoquesco Gorge where the river leaves the valley has prevented the normal downcutting of the Atoyac and allowed it to form a broad valley in the area of shallow gradient. This is completely unlike the Tehuacán Valley, which is a typical V-shaped Mexican montane valley, or even the Nochixtlán Valley, which has only a small

extent of shallow gradient near the upper limit of the drainage.

The Oaxaca Valley is bounded on the east by the confused masses of the Sierra Madre del Sur which, in this part of Mexico, still trend northwest–southeast. To the north, the Mixteca Alta, including the Nochixtlán Valley, forms a rugged but less elevated mass than the eastern ridges. To the west, more tumultous ridges gradually dissipate in the Mixteca Baja and the Pacific coast.

The rock formations of the surrounding mountains are a mixture of metamorphic rocks (gneiss is a dominant basement member), Cretaceous limestones, and Miocene ignimbrite (volcanic tuff) formations, all of which have contributed to the valley alluvium. For the archaeologist, the exposed ignimbrite formations on the walls of the Tlacolula arm of the valley near Mitla are particularly important, because this soft rock has become pocked with rock shelters, some of which were occupied in the early days of human occupation of the area (see Topic 5). The harder rocks of other parts of the valley slopes have contributed to the piedmont gravels.

In addition to the main rivers, some permanently flowing streams enter the valley primarily from the mountains to the northeast, but some also enter from the ridges to the west. As we shall see later, the effective moisture in the Oaxaca Valley is limited, and these tributary streams have been a source of irrigation water for cultivation on the piedmont and the outer edge of the high alluvium (see Topic 94).

Climate of the Oaxaca Valley

The Oaxaca Valley is a semiarid southern Mexican valley with a complex meteorological pattern, conditioned in part by the mountain masses surrounding it and in part by the trade winds that blow predominantly from one direction. The trade winds blowing inland from the Caribbean or, in this instance, from the Gulf of Mexico first encounter the high ridges of the Sierra Madre del Sur and lose their moisture adiabatically before reaching the Oaxaca Valley. The rainy season for the valley is roughly May through September when the trade winds are most active at this latitude. In general, rainfall at Oaxaca de Juárez ranges between 420 and 896 mm; this city is near the center of the valley where the two long arms of the wishbone join the base. Another recording station at Tlacolula records mean annual precipitation from 382 to 840 mm over a long span of years. Thus, although Tlacolula is higher (by 100 m) than Oaxaca, the rainfall is appreciably less in that arm of the valley, an important few millimeters of rain in an area of rainfall deficiency.

Temperature in the valley seldom drops to freezing in the northern arm and the western arm, but the increasing elevation into the eastern arm increases the danger of frost (Tlacolula has recorded as low as −8.5° C), placing a limit that is independent of rainfall to the growing season in that portion of the valley. Therefore, even though water might be available for irrigation in December and January, such crops as beans and maize might suffer from frost damage in the Tlacolula−Mitla−Matatlán region. Needless to say, the same danger exists for farmers whose cultivated plots are higher on the mountainsides surrounding the valley.

Vegetation of the Oaxaca Valley

The Oaxaca Valley is a typical Mexican valley in that the current vegetational cover provides little example for understanding the original vegetational cover for the area. The valley bottom has undoubtedly been cleared for thousands of years, although second growth valley forest may have persisted in patches nearly to the present time (one small woodlot was available for observation in the 1960s). It is certain, however, that all woody vegetation has been cut innumerable times to furnish structural material, tools, and fuel for the population—which must have reached high levels in prehistoric times, if we are to judge from the Classic and Postclassic centers. The original vegetation, however, can be reconstructed by comparison with the remnants of vegetation in the valley, in other parts of Mexico where population pressure has not been so great, and in other parts of tropical America where similar conditions prevail.

The original vegetation of the broad alluvial valley bottom is not difficult to reconstruct. Although the elevation was probably lower by several meters before the original forest was removed, the same conditions would have been present—the constantly flowing Río Atoyac with low levees, behind which were broad alluvial plains rising gradually toward the piedmont on either side. In this soil, the water table is only slightly below the ground level near the river, and it remains within the reach of the roots of trees for some distance back from the river. With the conditions then prevailing—hundreds-of-centuries-old soil profiles with heavy organic A horizons and a heavy forest cover to aid in absorbing and retaining annual precipitation—the valley bottom was a mesic habitat. Immediately along the Río Atoyac, where flood scouring would have disturbed the vegetation, willow and alder probably dominated. Removed from the waterside and partially protected by the levees, however, a fully developed evergreen tropical forest would have covered the valley. Genera undoubtedly included a large amount of *Ficus*, but also many representatives of the Lauraceae such as *Persea americana, Ocotea* spp., *Nectandra* spp., and *Litsea* spp., perhaps some Annonaceae including *Anona purpurea*, which now grows along watercourses higher on the valley sides, and any number of other tropical trees which prefer mesic cool habitats. The primary forest must have consisted of individual trees as large as 1.5 m in diameter at breast height and 30 m or more tall, growing 10−20 m apart. The canopy would have been closed, however, permitting very little sunlight to penetrate to the floor, which would have had a scattered cover of herbaceous plants and ferns. In the forest canopy, the limbs of the trees would have been nearly covered with epiphytic orchids, peperomias, ferns, and araceous vines. Undoubtedly, a number of lianes draped from the treetops, though all have now vanished because of opening of the forest habitat.

Away from the alluvial plain of the river valley, the water table would have been (and still is) inaccessible to many plants. This is precisely the habitat in which mesquite (*Prosopis juliflora*) flourishes. Prior to human disturbance, the evergreen valley forest was fringed by a band of mesquite forest which is represented today only by a very disturbed remnant in the Tlacolula arm of the valley near Mitla. On the upper alluvial area, which quickly exceeds the water table depth to which even mesquite roots can reach, the vegetation becomes a thorn scrub forest with many leguminous trees accented by columnar cacti (*Lemaireocereus* and *Myrtillocactus*) and prickly pear (*Opuntia* spp.). The thorn forest vegetation, with its many species, continues up the valley sides over the piedmont to about 1700 m. While this semiarid vegetation persists today in many parts of the Oaxaca Valley, and its extent may be greater now than in the Classic and Postclassic, it, too, must vary greatly from the vegetation zone the original agriculturists found. Many people today regularly harvest the thorn forest for its edible fruits, seeds, and shoots. It is heavily utilized for pasturing sheep and goats. Also, it has long been a source of firewood and durable wood for handles, structures, and so on. These human activities cannot fail to have changed the aspect of the thorn forest as well as the species composition.

At the upper edge of the thorn forest, oak trees, madroño, and *membrillo* (*Amelanchier denticulata*) begin to appear, marking the lower edge of the montane forest of oak and pine. In this higher elevation the rainfall is greater and, perhaps, spread over a longer season. Unfortunately, we have no meteorological records for this area. The vegetation, however, quickly assumes the aspect of oak–pine forest generally seen at higher elevations in southern Mexico. The early residents of the Oaxaca Valley exploited this area for acorns and piñon seeds (as evidenced by archaeological macroremains in Guilá Naquitz Cave) and for charcoal, so numerous changes have been made in this vegetational zone. For instance, a careful search failed to establish the presence today for piñon pine on the slopes above the valley, or of any person who remembers using or hearing about the use of piñones.

THE VALLEY OF NOCHIXTLÁN

The Nochixtlán Valley lies to the southwest of the Tehuacán Valley and to the north of the Oaxaca Valley. It is smaller in area than the other valleys discussed here, but was the site of the richest and most powerful *cacicazgo* in the Mixteca Alta (see Topic 73). The valley is the upper end of a drainage system that lies nearly on the Continental Divide (M. Kirkby 1972). The floor lies above 2100 m elevation and the surrounding ridges are at about 2500 m elevation. In general, the main drainage is to the south.

Because the geology of the Nochixtlán area plays a major part in the environmental modification in use in the valley, I shall review it briefly, following the discussion by M. Kirkby (1972). The most important formation is the "red to purple calcareous shales," which are the Yanhuitlán Beds. Probably a facies of this formation is the conglomerate Jaltepec Beds. The Jaltepec Beds are to the south and east of the main part of the valley, which lies mainly in the Yanhuitlán Beds. In the ridges of the northwest and northeast are Cretaceous limestones. The Yanhuitlán Beds are associated with Tertiary andesitic volcanic formations and a few exposures of interbedded ignimbrites and tuff.

The Yanhuitlán Beds are most important for the inhabitants of the valley because of the fertility of the soils. Because the valley is embedded in the formation, the side slopes and near ridge tops are all conditioned by the history of the calcareous shales. This rock is soft, friable, and easily formed by natural forces. The natural angle of repose of the Yanhuitlán Bed slopes is 50 to 60°, but the erodibility of the red beds results in particularly long erosion gullies. As M. Kirkby has pointed out, even the gullies have erosion gullies. Because the formation has a high calcareous content, soil formation under primary forest conditions produced an organically rich A horizon, a thick B horizon (probably gray), bounded next to the C horizon by a wide layer of calcareous accumulation. This material is often called caliche in other parts of Mexico and the southwestern United States. While the forest cover remained intact, the calcrete layer remained soft and permeable. Subsequent removal of the forest cover for cultivation or for fuel began a cycle of erosion that soon removed the upper soil layers exposing the calcrete. Upon exposure, the moist calcrete begins a hardening process which results in the formation of a soft calcareous rock impervious to rapid percolation and unsuitable for many species of plants. This soil, then, remains sparsely vegetated and completely unavailable for agriculture.

Climate of the Nochixtlán Valley

Unfortunately, the climatic records for this area are very few and very recent. Mean annual temperatures vary from 15.5 to nearly 17° C over the short period of record. As the valley lies at a high elevation, frost regularly occurs on the surrounding heights, and cold air masses sliding downslope may form frost pockets on the valley floor. The Nochixtlán station has recorded a temperature of −8° C. The regular occurrences of frost in the valley during December, January, or February would be expected at this elevation in spite of its location in the tropic zone. During most years, however, the rainy season is a frost-free period enabling crops of maize and beans to mature not only in the valley but up the slopes to elevations of 2600 m. This expansion of growing area is possible because of increasingly heavier and earlier rains at higher elevations.

The rainfall pattern of the Nochixtlán Valley is largely conditioned by the higher ridges to the north and east of the area; in other words, the Nochixtlán Valley is in their rainshadow. Isohyet maps have been prepared by the Comisión del Papaloapan for the years during which observations have been made at Nochixtlán. These maps show major parallel lines of isohyets along the mountain front to the east of the area, and generally a loop including the valley within a 600- to 900-mm isohyet. Mean annual rainfall recorded for Nochixtlán averages about 400–500 mm, with the major peak in June. A later peak may occur in September. As in other areas of southern Mexico, these precipitation peaks may be influenced by tropical storms passing close to either the Atlantic or Pacific coasts. With increasing elevation, the rainfall pattern shows an earlier beginning date for the rainy season and a generally larger mean annual rainfall. For instance, at 2600 m the rainy season begins in March and the mean annual rainfall is usually more than 1000 mm. Thus, maize may be seeded earlier at higher elevations (probably with varieties having shorter growing seasons) and a harvest assured, although maize generally cannot be sown on the floor of the valley until June.

Vegetation of the Nochixtlán Valley

As has been explained in an earlier publication (C. E. Smith 1976), direct observations may no longer be made of

the vegetation of the Nochixtlán area because it was removed before observations were recorded. Comparisons of
the surviving vegetation with other areas of Mexico at similar elevations and with similar climatic patterns, however,
suggest that the Nochixtlán Valley was originally completely covered with an oak–pine forest. Even on the valley
bottom, the rainfall is sufficient for the maintenance of a
forest cover, considering the richness of the soil derived from
the Yanhuitlán Red Beds and its water retention characteristics. Along the permanently flowing streams in the valley
bottom, willow and alder borders would have formed, with
mixed mesic forests further from the stream itself. On elevations where drainage was locally better, pine probably dominated; on rocky eminences with scant soil, a more xerophytic vegetation formed with *palo bobo* (*Ipomoea* sp.), prickly
pear (*Opuntia* spp.), huizache (*Acacia* sp.), juniper, and
other species that have invaded the waste areas today. Before
the original forest cover was removed, it is doubtful the
xerophytic species occupied very much of the Nochixtlán
area. It must always be remembered that under the original
forest cover, the absorptive qualities of the forest soils would
have attenuated the effects of the rainfall so that soils would
have had higher water tables and would have remained
moist longer in the early dry season. Also, stream flow
would have been attenuated by the greater absorption of
rainfall.

At the present time, the greater part of the valley bottom
and the lower slopes are open for agriculture, or the soil is
covered with a light cover of second growth vegetation,
which generally includes the morning glory tree, spiny
leguminous trees, prickly pear, and many species of weedy
plants. Higher on the slopes where agriculture is no longer
profitable, larger second growth trees include *guaje cimmar-
rón* (*Calliandra* sp.), *xunu ina* (*Cercocarpus pringlei*), and
occasionally common *guajé* (*Leucaena esculenta*). The latter
may have persisted from a former planting. Many of the
ridgetops are now capped with a caliche pavement, the soil
having long since eroded down to the formerly buried calcrete. The second growth vegetation on these areas frequently includes juniper (*Juniperus flaccida*), manzanita
(*Arctostaphylos pungens*), and several Labiateae (including
Satureja mexicana and *Salvia thymoides*), all widely spaced
so that abundant rocky surface shows between the plants.
The hedgerows between fields and around house com-
pounds frequently include *Lantana involucrata*, *Salvia semi-
strata*, *Agave ferox* (from which pulque is prepared), *Croton
gracilis* (canelilla), and *Condalia mexicana* (*espino
yunoyoco*).

THE VALLEY OF TEHUACÁN

The Tehuacán Valley lies to the southeast of the Valley of
Puebla and to the northeast of the Cañada de Cuicatlán. It is
a small valley trending northwest to southeast immediately
behind the ramparts of the Sierra Madre de Oaxaca. The
ridge immediately to the east of the valley is the Sierra de
Zongólica. The valley is drained by the Río Salado, which
originates largely in tributaries in the mountains to the

northeast. While the Río Salado is a permanent stream, at
the present time the flow is small even during the rainy season because so much water is removed for irrigation.

The Sierra Madre de Oaxaca along the northeastern side
of the Tehuacán Valley is composed of metamorphosed sedi-
mentary rocks, for the most part, and it furnishes an acidic
soil on that side of the valley. To the southwest, the principal
rock formations are travertines and limestones, which both
drain readily and provide an alkaline soil on the southwest
side of the valley. The valley slopes downward from the
northwestern end with two major cuestas providing giant
steps, one just to the south of Tehuacán and the other just to
the north of San Gabriel Chilac. At Tehuacán, the valley has
an elevation of 1676 m. It falls rapidly to the confluence of
the Río Salado with the Río Grande at about 600 m. The
valley thus spans climatic zones from temperate on the upper
end (with frost in the winter months) to tropical on the lower
end.

The unique feature of the geology of the Tehuacán Valley
is the issuing of five large springs from the travertine formation on the southwestern side of the city of Tehuacán. Major
upwellings occur at El Riego, San Lorenzo, Peñafiel, and
Garci Crespo. All of the springs are heavily charged with
mineral salts so that the outflowing water deposits a crust on
the bottom and sides of the stream bed. All of the large
springs have been, or are now being, used heavily as a source
of bottled water and soft drinks, and they have been widely
sought in the past as curative waters. These permanent water
sources have been an invaluable irrigation resource in a
semidesert valley.

Climate of the Tehuacán Area

The massive ridges of the Sierra Madre de Oaxaca to the
northeast of the valley rise to elevations of about 3000 m.
They effectively screen the interior valleys from the trade
winds that are forced, by adiabatic lifting, to shed their
water content on the Gulf side of the ranges. To the southwest, the lower Mixtec highlands and the distance from the
Pacific Ocean effectively reduce the amount of rainfall available from that direction. Thus, the Tehuacán Valley is an
area of deficient rainfall.

The precipitation in the area falls primarily in the period
from May until October, but the rainfall is not evenly dis-
tributed during this period. A series of showers at the beginning of the rainy season in May and June are sufficient to
germinate the seeds of maize and beans in the dry farming
areas. From the middle of July to the middle of August,
however, a dry period sets in during which little precipitation occurs. Thereafter, a more productive rainy season
peaks in September and tapers off through October. This
rainfall is generally sufficient to mature the crops which
were planted with the rainfall in May.

Altogether, the mean annual rainfall at Tehuacán is about
500 mm. Moving southward in the valley, the rainfall generally averages slightly higher, or about 600 mm annually.
One of the distressing things about rainfall in the valley is its
local nature. One section of the valley may have a cloudburst

during which several millimeters of rain fall (and rapidly run off) while not a drop falls anywhere else in the area. Just to the east of the crest of the Sierra, some areas record as much as 4000 mm mean annual rainfall.

The larger amounts of rainfall in the September period may be, in part, due to the large tropical weather disturbances that move onto the Gulf Coast of Mexico in some years. There is also a suspicion that tropical storms coming inland from the Pacific Ocean may provide some precipitation in the Tehuacán Valley. None of the precipitation added by tropical storms is dependable. Nor, in the short run, is the normal shower system. Over the rainy season, however, enough rainfall generally occurs to mature the special varieties of maize and beans that are grown by dry farming in the valley.

Original Vegetation

Reconstructing the original vegetation of the Tehuacán Valley is not as difficult as is the reconstruction of vegetation for an area like the Valley of Oaxaca because the Tehuacán Valley vegetation has never been completely removed at one time. Thus, seed sources have always been available for the revegetation of abandoned land. The human population of the area has undoubtedly been greater in the past than it is at the present. The climate and the topography of the valley, however, are such that it is doubtful that the entire area has been completely denuded. The credit for this does not go to the human population directly, but to the bountiful sources of water that made irrigation agriculture eminently successful during both dry and rainy seasons.

Above about 1700 m on the slopes of the Sierra Madre de Oaxaca, the original native vegetation was a pine–oak forest. Part of this forest still remains, but it is rapidly being removed for firewood and forest products and by clearing for farming. Some of the accessible oak forest on the slopes

above the valley appear to be little disturbed, and they have probably never been clear-cut.

Below the 1700 m line on the northeastern side of the valley, the vegetation consists of a thorn-scrub–cactus vegetation which is locally variable, but which is generally the same assortment of species along the entire length of the valley. Most of the trees are short with umbrella-shaped crowns; they belong primarily to the Leguminosae, Burseraceae, Bombacaceae, and other families notable for xerophytes. Most are microphyllous and deciduous. Conspicuous among the trees are large columnar cacti of a half-dozen genera. The largest of these is the candelabra-like *cardón* which bears edible fruit in April near the end of the dry season. Under the trees, spiny, straggling shrubs fill in open space, but the ground is mostly open, even during the rainy season; this is largely because of the large herds of sheep and goats that browse through the thorn scrub and that have undoubtedly altered the species composition of the herbaceous cover since they were introduced about 400 years ago. As primeval as the thorn-scrub vegetation looks today, it is certainly all secondary growth. Throughout the most mature-looking vegetation, one encounters foundations, evidence of clearings for agriculture, and other evidences of former human occupation.

Along the western side of the valley, the underlying travertine provides an alkaline soil which drains more readily than the soil along the eastern side of the valley. Furthermore, along the eastern side, streams from rainfall near the summit of the ridges provide more soil moisture than is available along the dry western side of the valley. The thorn-scrub vegetation along this side is much more open, with a few trees such as the arborescent *Ipomoea* (*palo bobo*) and the spiny *Fouquieria formosa* (*palo santo*). Cacti and magueys of all kinds are conspicuous. While it would seem that this desert landscape is a poor area for agriculture, fields are opened and cultivated with available moisture during the summer rainy period.

The Cañada de Cuicatlán

JOSEPH W. HOPKINS III

The Cañada de Cuicatlán, a long, narrow river canyon to the southeast of the Valley of Tehuacán, was the major Precolumbian route between Tehuacán and Oaxaca. Here the Río Salado, flowing south from Tehuacán, and the Río Grande, flowing north past Cuicatlán, join to produce the Santo Domingo, a major branch of the Río Papaloapan. My brief description of the environment is drawn from a longer work (Hopkins 1974).

THE CLIMATE OF THE CAÑADA

The large mountain mass of the Sierra Madre Oriental to the east of Cuicatlán removes much of the moisture from the

air before it reaches the Cañada. As a result, the Cañada receives on an average less than 300 mm of rain annually. The maximum rainfall usually comes in June, while in January and February no appreciable rain falls at all. In exceptional years, however, such as 1941 and 1969, as much as 300 mm, or the average expected for the entire year, may fall in a single month. In such years disastrous floods cut off communication out of the Cañada, washing out the road and railroad and carrying off riverside fields. In 1969, when I was in the field, railroad cranes dropped one-ton boulders in the river to shore up the embankments, only to have them carried away by the river.

The Cañada is well known throughout Mexico for its heat. The average annual temperature is 24.5° C, with a

maximum of 43.0 and a minimum of 6.0° C. The greatest
heat is in April and May before the rains begin, and the
lowest in the months from October to February. The average
in the warmest month (May) is 26.5° C and in the coldest
(February) the average is 22.6° C, not a large range. Since the
Cañada is a low basin surrounded by high mountain masses,
a cold air sink forms, and it becomes quite cool at night.

THE VEGETATION OF THE CAÑADA

Because of the hot, dry climate, the most common vegetation in the Cañada is a low, thorny forest composed of mixed
thorny trees and large cacti. Among the trees are palo verde
or *mantecoso* (*Cercidium praecox*), with its bright green
bark; mesquite (*Prosopis juliflora*); and quebracho (*Acacia
unijuga*). These are low trees, 6–10 m high. Another low tree
found farther up the slopes is the *pochote* (*Ceiba parvifolia*)
which fruits in pods that give a cotton-like kapok with edible
seeds. Mixed with these are the largest of the organ cacti, the
cardón (*Lemaireocereus weberi*). Other large cacti are the
pitahayo (*Lemaireocereus pruinosus*) and *pitahayo viejo*
(*Cephalocereus chrysacanthus*). Smaller cacti include the
quiotilla (*Escontria chiotilla*) and nopal (*Opuntia* sp.). In
and around Cuicatlán, because of extensive pasturing of
goats, there is often not much underbrush, and one can walk
through park-like aisles between the low trees and cacti in
open shade, only occasionally having to duck under low
branches. Farther from the town, however, and up the slope
from the floor of the Cañada, the undergrowth becomes
more closed, with sparse grass (*Pentarrhaphis polymorpha*),
the nettle-like *mala mujer* (*Jatropha urens*), and small barrel
cacti (*Mammillaria*). On the cliff above Cuicatlán one is
struck by the extensive cover of *pie de cabra* (*Solanum ama-
zonium*) with its pretty purple flowers—until one tries to
walk through these waist-high plants and finds out they are
quite spiny.

On the gravel bars along the edge of the Río Grande the
vegetation is more sparse because of the annual flooding.
Characteristic is the *palo de agua* (*Asianthus viminalis*), a
willow-like tree with soft, spongy wood. True willows (*Salix
chilensis*) also grow along the river. Small specimens of the
thorny scrub also invade the edges of the river. Along the

edge of the canal from the Río Grande that led to the sugar-
cane fields of La Iberia, I saw a large tree identified as *Pithecolobium dulce*. The specimen I observed was 10–15 m high
and 2–2.5 m in diameter, but despite its size, it was later
carried off without a trace in the floods of 1969.

In the bottoms of the canyons of the little tributary rivers
that supply the irrigation systems, and especially on the
somewhat larger but still restricted canyons of the headwa-
ters of the Río Grande and the Río de las Vueltas, is a more
humid microenvironment with much more lush tree and
brush vegetation. While the sides of the canyons will still be
covered with the same thorny scrub and cactus as previously
described, the canyon bottoms will support large trees, such
as the *chupandilla* (*Cyrtocarpa procera*), which has a sour
but tasty fruit with a large pit, and grows to 15 m long (I say
"long" because they frequently grow horizontally out over
the canyons, rather than up). Another tree that looks like
chupandilla with its white bark and long twisted roots is the
amate, also called *higo* or *capahuico*, which is a *Ficus* and, I
was told, is not used for anything, although in other parts of
Mexico its bark is used to make paper. Carrizo, or river
cane, often grows right at the river's edge. High on the Río
Chiquito de Cuicatlán is a single enormous chicozapote
(*Achras zapota*) which may be left from a small planting at
previous time. Other plants found are the tree
Pithecolobium dulce and the reed *Arundo donax*.

The thorn scrub grows up to about 1200 to 1400 m above
sea level on the eastern slope of the Cañada. At 1200 m, the
first oaks begin to appear. The first dry-farmed fields appear
at 1600 m. The lower oaks are *Quercus glaucophylla, Q.
glauccides,* and *Q. liebmannii*. These are low, stunted oaks,
pointed out to me by a Mexican botany student as curious
trees that drop and replace their leaves every year. Higher
up, *Quercus consperza* grows to 10 to 15 m high. Higher still
the pines mix with the oaks or form pure stands. Some of the
pines are *Pinus montezumae* and *P. oocarpa*. At present the
forests above the Cañada are being managed by the Pa-
pelería Tuxtepec, with nurseries and controlled cutting.
Oaks are being deliberately selected against, so I am not sure
how much of the stands of huge pines were natural or man-
influenced. A number of epiphytes, lichens, and mosses appear on the trunks of the oaks and pines in this more humid
environment.

TOPIC 4
Pleistocene Fauna of Early Ajuereado Type from Cueva Blanca, Oaxaca

KENT V. FLANNERY

Almost nothing is known of the Paleoindian period in the
state of Oaxaca. There have been isolated discoveries of
mammoth remains in the valleys of Tamazulapan (Aveleyra
1948) and Nochixtlán (see Topic 5), but none had associ-

ated artifacts. An isolated mammoth molar in a curio shop in
Oaxaca City is said to have come from Zaachila. A mas-
todon eroding from a trail near San Baltazar Guelavila in the
canyons east of Mitla showed no evidence of having been

dispatched by man. Perhaps the most extensive Pleistocene fossil deposit in the Valley of Oaxaca runs for several kilometers in the Arroyo de los Cuajilotes above Santa Cruz Etla, but the University of Michigan project was unable to find any associated flints. This deposit, which may well antedate man's arrival in the New World, has produced so much material that some villagers at Santa Cruz use proboscidean limb bones as furniture.

Our best clue to this period so far is a small collection of fauna from stratigraphic Zone F at Cueva Blanca, near Mitla in the eastern Valley of Oaxaca (see Topic 5). Zone F is a layer of indurated sand (formed from weathered and subsequently consolidated volcanic tuff) which at first appeared to be a sterile deposit at the base of the cave (Flannery [ed.] 1970:17). As a precaution, my coinvestigator Frank Hole decided to dig a series of 1-m squares down deeper into Zone F. In the process he discovered several lenses of animal bones which show definite evidence of burning and some signs of artificial fracture. It was immediately apparent that some of these animals differed from the modern fauna associated with Zones E–A at Cueva Blanca. Unfortunately, no artifacts were found in any of the Zone F lenses, nor did any of the tiny charcoal specks add up to a decent radiocarbon sample. Radiocarbon dates for Zone E, which overlay F, ranged between 9050 and 8100 B.C.; Zone F could thus be older than 10,000 B.C.

One of the first animals to come to light in Zone F was the Texas gopher tortoise, *Gopherus* cf. *berlandieri*. This large land tortoise frequents the plains of south Texas and northeast Mexico today, but does not range south of San Luis Potosí. Another significant member of the Zone F fauna was a fox whose bones were too large and rugose to be those of the gray fox (*Urocyon cinereoargenteus*) native to Oaxaca today. They would appear to belong to the genus *Vulpes* (red foxes), and may well be those of *Vulpes macrotis*, the kit fox, which today inhabits Durango and Coahuila in northern Mexico. Neither the gopher tortoise nor the kit fox occurs anywhere near Oaxaca today.

Zone F also includes genera native to both Oaxaca and northern Mexico. Particularly common in this category are cottontails (*Sylvilagus* spp.), jackrabbits (*Lepus* sp.), and wood rats (*Neotoma* spp.). Deer of the genus *Odocoileus* (probably the white-tailed deer *O. virginianus*, although the sample is small) are also present. The microfauna, only partially analyzed at this writing, includes the murine opossum *Marmosa canescens*. There are also numerous birds in the songbird size range, whose species may eventually be identified.

COMPARISONS WITH TEHUACÁN

The Pleistocene fauna which most closely resembles that from Cueva Blanca F is the Early Ajuereado phase fauna from Zones XXV to XXVIII of Coxcatlán Cave in the Tehuacán Valley (Flannery 1967:140–144). That collection

of 1200 identifiable bones included animals no longer present in the Tehuacán Valley, as follows:

Common name	Scientific name	Number of fragments
Horse	*Equus* sp. (now extinct)	7
Pronghorn antelope	*Antilocapra americana*	45
Large jackrabbits	*Lepus* sp. (not *mexicanus*)	700+
Fox	Genus *Vulpes*, perhaps *V. macrotis*	49
Chipmunk-sized ground squirrel		4
Gopher tortoise	*Gopherus* cf. *berlandieri*	102
Quail	Not *Colinus* sp.	2

Fortunately, in the case of the Early Ajuereado fauna a few flint artifacts were found in association. There was also evidence for communal rabbit drives, with nearly 400 rabbit bones occurring in Zone XXVI alone; these included the trimmed-off feet of no fewer than 40 rabbits, most of which were found in a single 1-m square (Flannery 1966:802). Our conclusion was that the Late Pleistocene environment of Tehuacán was a temperate steppe, cooler and drier than today, and that the Early Ajuereado fauna withdrew to the north as temperatures rose and vegetation thickened in post-Pleistocene times.

According to James Schoenwetter (personal communication), pollen samples from Cueva Blanca F may also reflect a climate somewhat cooler than today's. Pine pollen dominates the sample, and there are occasional grains of spruce, fir, and elm. Pollen of mesquite, columnar cacti, *Agave*, and other thorn forest plants, however, is much more common than that of spruce or fir, and suggests that a thorn forest like the current one occurred not far from the cave. Perhaps the presumed cooler winter temperatures of the Pleistocene merely lowered the altitude at which the various Oaxacan vegetation zones occurred. Under such conditions, the mountain slopes near Cueva Blanca might have had pine forest; the piedmont a kind of thorn forest; and the alluvial valley floor a cover of mesquite, with mesophytic stands of willow and alder along the watercourses. Some northern Mexican species—like gopher tortoise, antelope, black-tailed jackrabbit, and kit fox—might have reached the Puebla–Oaxaca highlands during that climatic regime, withdrawing to the north when temperatures rose at the end of the Pleistocene. By 8900 B.C., the flora and fauna of the Valley of Oaxaca were essentially "modern," and apparently remained so up to the Spanish introduction of Old World species.

It is hard to know precisely how to deal with the Cueva Blanca F material. Since it was unaccompanied by artifacts, it can hardly be assigned to a meaningful cultural phase. It is more than just a Pleistocene faunal collection, on the other hand, since the evidence for burning is unequivocal and the bone percentages suggest human food preparation. In this respect the collection is reminiscent of the material from Coxcatlán Cave XXV–XXVIII, where only 11 identifiable artifacts were found with 1200 identifiable bones (Mac-Neish, Nelken-Terner, and Johnson 1967:Table 32). Obviously, such meager artifactual evidence precludes the sim-

ple solution, which would be to assign Cueva Blanca F to the Early Ajuereado phase; although the two faunas are undeniably similar, future discoveries might show that the associated artifacts are not. For the purposes of this volume, therefore, we will simply refer to the remains from Cueva Blanca F as late Pleistocene.

TOPIC 5
Excavated Sites of the Oaxaca Preceramic

KENT V. FLANNERY
RONALD SPORES

Between 8900 and 2000 B.C., the forested mountains and valleys of Oaxaca were occupied by small, scattered bands of Indians who hunted deer and peccary with atlatl darts tipped with flint projectile points; trapped rabbits, quail, and doves with snares; roasted maguey hearts in rock-lined earth ovens; harvested acorns, piñon nuts, cactus fruits, grass seeds, and a tremendous variety of native vegetable foods with baskets and carrying nets; and cooked over hearths kindled with fire drills.

Some time between 8000 and 5000 B.C. these Indians gradually brought a few species of vegetable foods into cultivation. One of those was a member of the squash–pumpkin taxon *Cucurbita pepo*, whose putative wild ancestor (*Cucurbita texana*) is not native to Oaxaca today[1]; but one wonders, because the Texas gopher tortoise reached Oaxaca during the late Pleistocene, whether *C. texana*'s range might once have extended farther to the south. Another plant belonged to the genus *Zea*, which includes both domestic maize (*Zea mays*) and its closest relative, teosinte (*Zea mexicana*). One current theory holds that teosinte, which has been reported from Oaxaca (Wilkes 1972), is the wild ancestor of maize (Galinat 1971; Beadle 1972). By 5050 B.C. at least 18 cobs of undisputed maize had been eaten at Coxcatlán Cave in the Tehuacán Valley, only 80 km from Yanhuitlán (Mangelsdorf, MacNeish, and Galinat 1967). While the addition of domestic plants to the diet did not initially change the lifeways of the Indians of Oaxaca, it set in motion a chain of events that would have a significant impact by 1500 B.C.

Our major source of data on this period is a series of caves, rock shelters, and open-air sites in the eastern Valley of Oaxaca and the Valley of Yanhuitlán–Nochixtlán (see Figure 2.2). Some of the caves are sufficiently dry to have desiccated plant remains from the period 8900 to 2000 B.C., while other sites have yielded pollen from important plants. In this topic we will present an inventory of excavated or tested sites. In later sections, Flannery will attempt to construct a chronology for Preceramic Oaxaca and to draw comparisons with the much more extensive Preceramic excavations of Mac-

Neish in the Tehuacán Valley (MacNeish, Nelken-Terner, and Johnson 1967).

PRECERAMIC SITES IN THE VALLEY OF OAXACA

Near Mitla, at the eastern limits of the Valley of Oaxaca, the landscape is dominated by high mountains, rocky cliffs, and mesas of Miocene volcanic tuff or ignimbrite (Williams

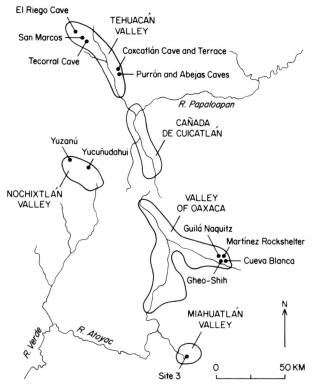

FIGURE 2.2. The valleys of Tehuacán, Cuicatlán, Nochixtlán, Oaxaca, and Miahuatlán, showing excavated Preceramic sites and important Preceramic surface finds.

---

and Heizer 1965). There are numerous caves and rock shelters in this formation, as well as veins of silicified ignimbrite which can be chipped into tools as readily as flint or chert. Since 1966, both caves and open-air sites of the preceramic hunting-and-gathering period have been investigated by the University of Michigan, with chipped stone analysis by Frank Hole; faunal analysis by Kent Flannery and Jane Wheeler; botanical analysis by C. Earle Smith, Jr., Paul Mangelsdorf, Thomas Whitaker, Lawrence Kaplan, and Jonathan Sauer; and palynology by James Schoenwetter and Suzanne K. Fish (Flannery [ed.] 1970).

Guilá Naquitz Cave

Guilá Naquitz Cave is a small shelter at the base of a large ignimbrite cliff, rising high above the valley floor some 5 km northwest of Mitla. The cliff occurs at an elevation of 1926 m above sea level (nearly 300 m above the valley floor) and faces southeast toward the town of Mitla. The cave lies near one of the main footpaths through the Dan Ro' Mountain range between Mitla and Díaz Ordaz (Santo Domingo del Valle).

Guilá Naquitz lies in a vegetation belt which contains the greatest variety of edible wild products in the vicinity of Mitla. This belt, which runs from about 1850–2000 m above sea level, includes scattered oaks (*Quercus* spp.), guaje (*Leucaena*), *Cassia, Acacia, Mimosa*, copal (*Bursera*), maguey (*Agave* spp.), *Bromelia, Dasylirion*, organ cactus (*Lemaireocereus, Myrtillocactus*), ocotillo (*Fouquieria*), cholla and nopal (*Opuntia*), *chapuliztle* (*Dodonaea*), *mala mujer* and *susí* (*Jatropha* spp.), nanche (*Malpighia*), wild onions (*Allium* sp.), and wild black zapote (*Diospyros*). On the plain below, near the Río Mitla, grow mesquite (*Prosopis juliflora*) and hackberry (*Celtis*).

The wild plants harvested by the Preceramic occupants of the cave, with one exception, can still be found in the area between Guilá Naquitz and the Río Salado. The lone exception is the nut of the piñon pine, a tree which is prized by charcoal-burners and may well have been lumbered out of the area. Pollen studies by Schoenwetter (1974) indicate that the plant environment of the Mitla region between 8900 and 6700 B.C. was similar enough to today's that the modern vegetational associations can be used as a guide to the past.

Prehistoric fauna of the area included white-tailed deer (*Odocoileus virginianus*) and collared peccary (*Dicotyles tajacu*), both of which are rare today because of hunting and deforestation. Small game is still abundant in the area and includes cottontails (*Sylvilagus cunicularis* and *S. floridanus*), opossums (*Didelphis marsupialis*), raccoons (*Procyon lotor*), cacomistles (*Bassariscus*), skunks (*Mephitis macroura*), and doves (*Zenaida asiatica* and *Zenaidura macroura*). Small rodents are numerous and include *Sigmodon hispidus, Neotoma mexicana, Liomys irroratus, Oryzomys* sp., *Peromyscus maniculatus, Baiomys musculus*, and *Reithrodontomys fulvescens*.

M. Kirkby and Whyte (n.d.) have divided the area between Guilá Naquitz and the Río Mitla into four vegetational zones, each of which has several facies depending on species dominance. Thorn Forest A, in which the cave occurs, has *Cassia* abundant, *Agave* common, and oaks present. Thorn Forest B, downslope, has oaks absent, *Cassia* less common, and *Ferrocactus* abundant. Mesquite Grassland A has abundant columnar cactus but only infrequent mesquite (*Prosopis*). Mesquite Grassland B, near the river, has mesquite as its dominant species. While this latter zone is a 4-km walk from the cave, it was probably second only to Thorn Forest A in importance. This is the zone of alluvium where mesquite yields 184 kg of edible portion per hectare, and where village life eventually arose after agriculture had developed further (Flannery 1973:298). Almost certainly, hunters and gatherers camped at places like Gheo-Shih in Mesquite Grassland B during the rainy season (July–August), moving up to Guilá Naquitz during the autumn (September–December) when the resources of Thorn Forest A were at their peak. By February, the Mitla area is in the grip of the dry season, and it would have been time to move again, possibly farther up into the oak–pine zone of the mountains to sites like Yuzanú (see below).

Guilá Naquitz was a shallow site; deposits reached about 120 cm depth in the rear and about 40 cm depth near the talus. Stratigraphy was very complex, but also very clear, as the color changes were quite dramatic and easy to follow. In the course of excavation, all projectile points, bifaces, scrapers, grinding stones, cordage, nets, fire-drills, or other items were recorded three-dimensionally (depth, distance from north, distance from west) so that the pattern of floor debris could be reconstructed. Preservation of plant materials was excellent in the 64-m² area protected by the overhanging cliff.

During 1966, eight zones or living floors were distinguished at Guilá Naquitz. Two of these (Zones A and super-A) belonged to Monte Albán IV and V, discussed in a later section (Topic 62). The lower six floors (Zones E, D, C, B3, B2, and B1) were Preceramic; radiocarbon dates are given in Table 2.1.

Zone E This was a layer of reddish-yellow sand which was found throughout the northern half of the site, but present in the southern half only in places. Most of the matrix was weathered ignimbrite, but it also contained chipped stone tools and plant remains left by small groups of people during very short stays. Deer and rabbit bone were present. Acorns were very abundant. Piñon nuts, mesquite, hackberry, *Opuntia* seeds, and chewed maguey quids were common, suggesting an occupation in the September–November period. A single unfinished projectile point, bifacial and unifacial scrapers, and numerous retouched flakes were present. The maximum thickness of the zone was 20 cm.

Zone D This was a layer of soft, dark gray ash, present in all squares near the rear of the cave, but absent or very reduced near the front. One of its features (Feature 3) was a pit containing a stone mano, an abrader, and acorns. Two other shallow pits in the same zone (Features 2 and 10) also had acorns, and these seeds were abundant elsewhere in the

TABLE 2.1.
Radiocarbon Dates for Preceramic Components in Oaxaca

Provenience	Date (Years B.C.)[a]	Lab. and No.[b]
Yuzanú, North cluster	2000 ± 200	W–480
Yuzanú, Roasting pit	2100 ± 200	W–479
Cueva Blanca, Zone D	2800 ± 190	M–2092
Cueva Blanca, Feature 18	3295 ± 105	GX–0782
Cueva Blanca, Zone D	[7250 ± 190]	SI–512
Guilá Naquitz, Zone B2	6670 ± 160	SI–515
Guilá Naquitz, Zone B2	6910 ± 180	GX–0784
Guilá Naquitz, Zone C	[4030 ± 220]	M–2100
Guilá Naquitz, Zone C	7280 ± 120	GX–0873
Guilá Naquitz, Zone C	7450 ± 300	M–2097
Guilá Naquitz, Zone D	[2350 ± 180]	M–2098
Guilá Naquitz, Zone D	7840 ± 240	GX–0783
Guilá Naquitz, Zone D	8750 ± 350	M–2099
Guilá Naquitz, Zone E	[4350 ± 220]	M–2101
Guilá Naquitz, Zone E	[5545 ± 90]	GX–0872
Cueva Blanca, Zone E	8100 ± 350	M–2093
Cueva Blanca, Feature 15	8780 ± 220	SI–511R
Cueva Blanca, Feature 15	8960 ± 80	SI–511
Cueva Blanca, Feature 15	9050 ± 400	M–2094

[a] Dates given in brackets are considered unacceptable.
[b] W = U.S. Geological Survey; M = University of Michigan; GX = Geochron Laboratories; SI = Smithsonian Institution.

debris. In some places, the matrix of Zone D had turned chocolate brown because of large numbers of burned oak leaves; it appeared that these had been brought into the cave as bedding. Average depth of debris in Zone D was 20 cm, and it may have represented the single autumn encampment (September–November) of a small group of people. Scrapers (both bifacial and unifacial), choppers, steep denticulate scrapers, and manos were common tools recovered. Deer, rabbit, and mud turtle were the dominant animal remains. Besides the abundant acorns, plant foods included mesquite, *susí*, nanche, piñon nuts, hackberry, *guaje*, nopal, prickly pear fruit, maguey, and wild onions. Also present were small, wild black runner beans (*Phaseolus*) and a single cucurbit seed thought to be from *Cucurbita pepo* (Whitaker n.d.). Radiocarbon dates for this zone indicate a date of 8750–7840 B.C., making this Oaxaca's oldest cucurbit seed.

Zone C This was a thick (20 cm) layer of almost pure white ash, underlain by an adherent strip of gritty brown to black compost; this zone was found throughout the cave. In some squares it became wispy and hard to trace, but in others it was quite prominent. The gritty black compost appeared to be mainly decomposed oak leaves. Zone C represented the single encampment of a small band of people made during the September–November period. Artifacts were like those in Zone D, but scarcer. Acorns, piñon nuts, maguey quids, hackberry seeds, and other plants were represented. It looked as if the group had begun the occupation by coating the floor of the cave with oak leaves and grass as bedding. Later, this bedding (as well as the accumulated plant material above it) had caught fire and smouldered. The

white ash appeared to be hearth material that had become widely spread around. Seeds of *Cucurbita pepo* were present and have been identified by Thomas Whitaker; Lawrence Kaplan has identified wild runner beans from Zone C. Also in this level, Schoenwetter (1974) has identified *Zea* pollen which is in the size range for teosinte—the putative ancestor of cultivated maize, according to one view.

Zones B, B1, B2, B3 These were the remains of a very thick and intensive series of repeated (possibly continuous) occupations by a fairly small band during the autumn season. Each occupation had produced a thin, floury layer of gray or white ash, and so little time had elapsed between occupations that the beds coalesced in places. For example, in the F row of squares, there was simply one stratum, Zone B. In other places, this stratum thickened and bifurcated into a zone B1 and a Zone B2 + B3. In some of the squares near the rear of the cave (e.g. the C and D rows of squares), this latter zone in turn bifurcated into a Zone B2 and a Zone B3. Much of the ash appeared to be hearth material that had been kicked around. Pollen was well preserved in it, as were plant remains and such things as knotted nets, basket fragments, and wooden artifacts (some of which may have been trap fragments). Many knots in maguey fiber were present, some of which appear to have been for carrying bundles of plant material to the cave. The abundant plant remains included acorns, piñon nuts, hackberry seeds, maguey quids, *susí* nuts, nanche, nopal, prickly pear fruit, mesquite, and *guaje*. White-tailed deer, cottontail rabbits of two species, and mud turtles were the most common faunal remains. In this series of zones, wild runner beans (*Phaseolus* sp.) and domesticated cucurbits (*C. pepo*) were more common than in lower zones. One Pedernales projectile point and a number of scrapers and choppers, as well as grinding stones, showed up in the debris. Artifacts, however, were not as abundant at Guilá Naquitz as they were in most of the Tehuacán caves (e.g., Coxcatlán Cave). Radiocarbon dates indicate an age of 6910–6670 B.C. for Zone B2.

Cueva Blanca

This is a large cave in an ignimbrite cliff 4 km northwest of Mitla, at an elevation of 1813 m, just at the present lower limits of the oak tree zone. The area below the overhang is 11 m by 15 m, but due to its western exposure and a sloping ceiling which rises to 5 m in front, rain enters it and preservation is poor. The cave faces west over an arroyo which lies 14 m below; the slopes are covered with *guaje* (*Leucaena*), *Mimosa*, *Acacia*, copal (*Bursera*), *Jatropha* (*mala mujer* and *susí*), wild onions (*Allium*), prickly pear, organ cactus, maguey, and *Dodonaea*.

Excavations in 1966 were begun by Flannery and completed by Frank Hole. Seventy-five 1-m squares in the rear three-fourths of the cave (where preservation was best and stratigraphy clearest) were excavated, wholly by individual living floors. Soft upper layers were excavated solely by trowel, screwdriver, and paint brush, while the Pleistocene layer at the base (Zone F) was indurated ignimbrite sand and had to be excavated with digging bars. All retouched tools recognized in the field were plotted three-dimensionally, and chipping debris was counted by 1-m square. Back-plotting of the three-dimensionally recorded tools revealed that the Preceramic occupation floors were slightly basin-shaped, in spite of the fact that the natural layers (each with its distinct color and texture) in which they occurred appeared horizontal. This situation had occurred because the bulk of the matrix was fine particles of volcanic tuff weathered from the roof, and not cultural debris. Near the front of the cave, where rain had repeatedly penetrated, the cultural stratigraphy was unreadable and the deposits had a uniform gray color from top to bottom. Only the lowest four zones (F, E, D, and C) were Preceramic. Zone F was apparently Pleistocene in age and has already been described in Topic 4.

Zone E This was a layer of gray ash with charcoal flecks, averaging only 15–20 cm thick and occupying only a portion of the area excavated, probably the remains of a small group during a brief occupation. At least one hearth (Feature 15) appeared, yielding three radiocarbon samples dated to between 9050 B.C. and 8780 B.C. The small number of tools included a few projectile points, side-scrapers, and retouched flakes. Deer and cottontail were represented, all species being those which occur in the area today.

Zone D This was a layer of tan-gray or salmon-colored ash which (originally) filled the entire excavated area of the cave and reached a thickness of 25–40 cm. This was probably the remains of a somewhat longer (winter, deer-hunting?) camp by a group of five to eight persons. White-tailed deer were butchered in the northeast quadrant of the cave, and nine projectile points and hundreds of flint chips accompanied them. Like the Abejas phase in the Tehuacán Valley, this occupation has Tilapa, La Mina, Trinidad, and San Nicolás points, and well-made bifaces. A hearth, Feature 18, intrusive into Zone E evidently was dug down from D; it gave a ^{14}C date of 3295 B.C. Charcoal from elsewhere in Zone D gave a date of 2800 B.C., also suggesting a date contemporary with the Abejas phase.

Zone C A layer of white ash (and considerable ignimbrite sand) some 20–40 cm thick covered most of the excavated area. The occupation was similar to that in Zone D, but produced fewer artifacts and may have been of somewhat shorter duration; most of the matrix, especially around the edges of the living floor, is naturally weathered ignimbrite. The hunting of deer and cottontail and collecting of mud turtle seem to be the activities best represented, and tools include one-hand manos, scrapers, bifaces, and projectile points of the Coxcatlán, La Mina, Hidalgo, and Trinidad types.

Gheo-Shih

Gheo-Shih (Zapotec; in Spanish, *Río de las Jícaras*) is an open-air Preceramic camp site in a modern maguey field 4 km west of Mitla. It lies on an alluvial fan flanked by two dry arroyos near the north bank of the Mitla River, at an altitude of 1660 m. Underlying Gheo-Shih is a layer of indurated

sand alluvium, apparently an older flood plain of the river, which is exposed in very few places today. Because this older alluvium is generally covered by recent alluvial deposits, few Preceramic sites of this type have been found. Gheo-Shih appears to be an example of what MacNeish (1964) has called a "seasonal macroband camp."

The site occupies an area about 100 by 150 m, or around 1.5 ha. The surface and the dry arroyos to either side were littered with metate and mano fragments, bifaces, scraper planes, and projectile points of La Mina, Trinidad, and San Nicolás types. Most frequent, however, was the Pedernales type (with a concave-based stem), present also in uppermost levels at Guilá Naquitz Cave, and occurring as a "rare" element in sites of the Coxcatlán phase in Tehuacán. It appears that Gheo-Shih may have been a summer encampment made along the Mitla River in what is today Mesquite Grassland B by a much larger group of people than those who had occupied Guilá Naquitz in the autumn. It therefore provided us with an opportunity to study a different "structural pose" in the annual shifting settlement system of the Preceramic hunters and gatherers of the eastern Valley of Oaxaca.

Gheo-Shih was studied during 1967 by Frank Hole. The first stage was a controlled surface collection. Hole and his assistants laid out a grid of 5-by-5-m squares over the entire surface of the site and undertook a total surface pickup. All artifacts and unworked stone were collected and analyzed by 5-m squares; all projectile points, bifaces, choppers, metates, manos, and so on were plotted two-dimensionally on the master map of the site. Numbers of waste flakes and fire-cracked rocks were recorded by square, and a contour map drawn showing concentrations of various kinds of tools over the entire surface of the site. On the basis of the completed map, Hole and his assistants were able to detect areas with high concentrations of grinding implements, other areas with abundant points and scrapers, and so on.

The second step was the testing of areas on Gheo-Shih which appeared to be functionally distinct. Testing was conducted by 1-m squares, placed so as to sample various areas which appeared (on the basis of surface material) to be different from one another. The fifth test square yielded evidence of architecture of an unusual type, and this area was exposed to an extent of over 150 m².

The architecture consisted of two parallel rows of boulders about 20 m long (Figure 2.3). The space between them, which was 7 m wide, was swept clean and contained virtually no artifacts. To either side of the parallel lines of boulders, however, artifacts were abundant. The boulder lines ended without turning a corner, and their function is unknown. What they most resemble are the borders of a cleared "dance ground," such as characterized macroband camps of some Great Basin hunting–gathering Indian groups (see Flannery and Marcus 1976a: Fig. 10.1; Drennan 1976a: Fig. 11.11).

One other area of Gheo-Shih, to the north, was of interest because it had an unusually high concentration of tools for hunting and butchering, and yielded a number of ornaments of drilled stone (mostly pendants). The making of pendants

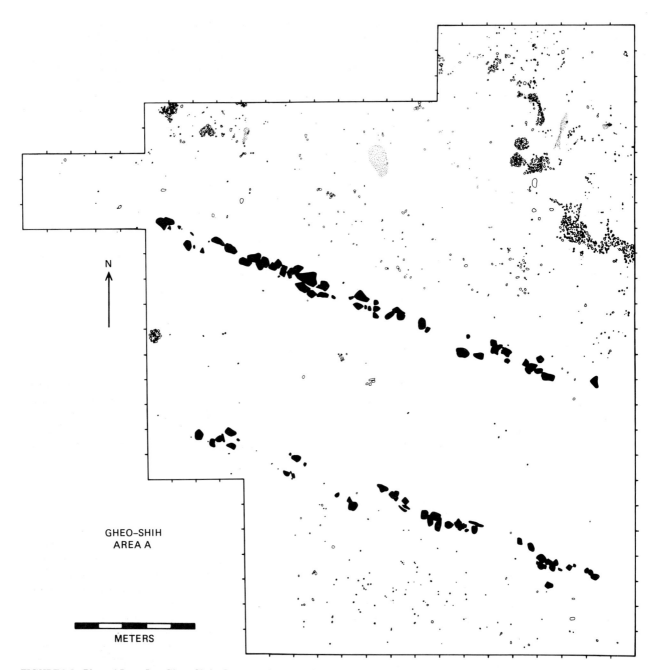

FIGURE 2.3. Plan of Area A at Gheo-Shih, Oaxaca, showing cleared area flanked by parallel lines of boulders. (Drawing by Frank Hole.)

from flat river pebbles may have been one localized activity on the site.

There were two disappointing aspects of the work at Gheo-Shih. One was a lack of plant and animal remains, since the site was so shallow and close to the surface that all organic materials had been leached out or decomposed. The second was a virtual lack of charcoal for radiocarbon dating. On typological grounds, Gheo-Shih should fall in the neighborhood of 5000 to 4000 B.C.

Pollen, however, was present at Gheo-Shih and is being analyzed by James Schoenwetter. Although not yet complete, the study so far shows pollen of maize or teosinte type. The location of Gheo-Shih is one that would be appropriate for rainy-season cultivation along the river floodplain, combined with collection of mesquite beans and other plant foods available on the alluvium during the summer.

The large sample of Preceramic tools from Gheo-Shih, coupled with analyses of their distribution over the site (and

of the very different activity areas present in the areas tested), should greatly increase our understanding of the internal structure of macroband camps.

Martínez Rock Shelter

This is a shelter 600 m north of Guilá Naquitz Cave, in the
same volcanic tuff cliff. The shelter runs 30 m north–south
and has an overhang of about 3 m; it is very irregular, following the cliff. The Martínez Rock Shelter has an excellent
platform and talus, facing east over the valley of Mitla at an
elevation of approximately 1920 m. Although it lies along
the main footpath through the mountains between Mitla
and Díaz Ordaz, the shelter seemingly never had heavy occupation. Local vegetation is the same as at Guilá Naquitz,
but plants were preserved only in Postclassic levels and features. Only the lower two stratigraphic zones, C and B, were
Preceramic, and neither of these was a true "living floor."

Flannery excavated about 17 m² of this rock shelter in
March 1966, but work ended when it became clear that no
preserved plant remains or animal bones were present in the
Preceramic levels. Techniques of excavation were the same
as those described for Guilá Naquitz and Cueva Blanca, and
work proceeded by "natural" strata (which were relatively
clear under the overhang, but less clear on the talus). All
projectile points, bifaces, scrapers, manos, metates, mortar,
and/or stone bowl fragments were mapped in place; however, the distributional patterns may not be meaningful for this
site because it appeared that, on the talus at least, rainwater
and soil creep have been gradually moving the lighter tools
downslope toward the level area below the shelter and leav-
ing the heavier ones behind.

Zone D This was a basal zone of sterile, weathered ignimbrite, palynologically "late Pleistocene" in age.

Zone C This was a layer of black earth with some rockfall,
containing flint tools not unlike those from lower Cueva
Blanca and lower Guilá Naquitz. Zone C was of varying
thickness (up to 30 cm) and could in no sense be considered a
"living floor." No plants, animal bones, or charcoal had
been preserved, and the black color seemed to come from the
decomposition of roots of modern vegetation growing on
the talus. Martínez bifaces (a distinctive, ovoid, bifacially
chipped tool) were the only clues to the date of this layer, as
they occurred also at Cueva Blanca, Guilá Naquitz, and
Gheo-Shih.

Zone B This was a brown earth layer, up to 30 cm thick,
resembling Zone C in most respects but of a different color.
Zone B was riddled with modern rootlets and had no preservation of plants, bones, or charcoal from the prehistoric era.
The density of flint tools was somewhat greater in this zone,
but it could not accurately be described as a living floor
either. Diagnostic tools included manos, metates, mortars or
crude stone bowls, crude blades, Martínez bifaces, cores,
scraper planes, end- and side-scrapers, flakes with edge polish (like "corn gloss" or "sickle sheen"), and very few projectile point fragments. The assemblage suggested a plant

collecting and processing camp rather than a hunting station, and our tentative conclusion is that the flakes with edge
polish were used to cut up maguey for roasting.

Because it appears that both Zones C and B accumulated
more from natural weathering processes than as living
floors, the Martínez Rock Shelter is of limited utility for
some archaeological purposes. Ironically, this very aspect
made it ideal for pollen analysis. Selecting a square with no
rootlet intrusion, Schoenwetter took a series of 14 pollen
samples at 5-cm intervals from the surface to 65-cm depth.
Pollen was beautifully preserved, and on the basis of correla-
tions with nearby sites through discriminant analysis, seems
to span almost the entire period of the Preceramic in the
Mitla area (Schoenwetter, personal communication). Various samples match up with Cueva Blanca E, Guilá Naquitz
C-B, Gheo-Shih, and Cueva Blanca D-C, all in proper stratigraphic order. Finally, the uppermost 10 cm of Zone B at
the Martínez Rock Shelter may represent the final stage of
the local Preceramic.

PRECERAMIC SITES IN THE MIXTECA

At present, the only excavated site in the Mixteca that has
yielded possible Preceramic remains is a hearth and associated cluster of artifacts and debitage in Paraje Yuzanú (a
Spanish corruption; the Mixtec would be *Yuzanuu*) in the
Yanhuitlán-Nochixtlán Valley of the Mixteca Alta (Lorenzo
1958a).

Yuzanú

Yuzanú is an open-air aceramic site in the profile of a
barranca some 2 km north-northeast of the city of
Yanhuitlán. Lying at an altitude of 2140 m, the site is in an
area which would once have been oak–pine forest (C. E.
Smith 1976). Settlement evidently took place on a layer of
sterile alluvium at the edge of a small stream which was
flowing at that time. Later erosional deposits buried the site,
probably as the result of intensive slope erosion which has
caused the rapid buildup of soils in areas such as Yanhuitlán,
Suchixtlán, and Nochixtlán, where Postclassic remains are
found under 3 to 4 m of alluvium. The artifact-bearing layer
at Yuzanú was eventually exposed again when the water
table dropped and the stream downcut, revealing what appeared to be a hearth in the A zone of a paleosol at the depth
of 7 m in the barranca profile.

In 1955, José Luis Lorenzo (1958a) exposed about 28 m²
of occupation floor at Yuzanú. The two most distinctive
features were the hearth and a nearby extensive scatter of
rocks with patches of ash. These rocks, some fire-cracked,
were not stream pebbles but chunks of volcanic tuff brought
in from a kilometer upstream. Lorenzo found 8 flint tools
and 50 pieces of chipping debris, all plotted by the Cartesian

coordinate system which he prefers to the American grid method. Two cores, two crude blades, and many waste flakes were found near the hearth; two scrapers, a core, and a use-retouched triangular flake were found in a scatter 3 m to the north. Both the hearth and the north tool cluster yielded charcoal with a radiocarbon date of 2100–2000 B.C. (see Table 2.1).

These relatively recent dates raise the question of whether Yuzanú is truly Preceramic or merely "aceramic." As one of us (Spores) pointed out during the Santa Fe seminar, they fall "perilously close" to a date of 1350 B.C. obtained for Early Cruz phase ceramics at Yucuita in the same valley (see Appendix). They also fall close to the earliest date (1925 B.C.) for Purrón phase pottery in the Tehuacán Valley (Johnson and MacNeish 1972:Table 4). As Flannery pointed out at the seminar, however, it is unlikely that we will ever be able to draw a hard and fast boundary between the Preceramic period and the earliest appearance of ceramics; Purrón pottery is too rare, and may appear at varying times in neighboring valleys.

Also at the seminar, Flannery expressed his opinion that the Yuzanú "hearth" is actually a maguey-roasting pit like those found in the Tehuacán caves or at Guilá Naquitz (e.g., Feature 7). The Yuzanú feature (Figure 2.4) is very large (2.4 m in diameter, 1 m deep) and has the same alternating layers of fire-cracked rocks (3 layers) and ash (4 layers) seen in maguey-roasting pits from the Mitla caves (Lorenzo 1958a:Fig. 17). In such pits, maguey hearts are roasted over heated rocks under a cover of maguey leaves and earth. When the cooking process is over, the rocks are removed, and they accumulate as a scatter like the one seen at Yuzanú. Such an interpretation would also explain the lack of projectile points and the predominance of cutting–scraping tools (for trimming maguey hearts) at Yuzanú.

Other Possible Sites

Numerous localities containing broken stone and charcoal fragments are observable along the high alluvial banks of Nochixtlán Valley streams, but none can be said to constitute a clearly discernible focus of Preceramic cultural ac-

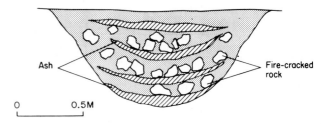

FIGURE 2.4. Cross-section of probable maguey roasting pit at Yuzanú, Oaxaca. (Redrawn from Lorenzo 1958a: Figure 17.)

tivity. Similar remains lying on or near the surface have not been distinguished from Ceramic period remains. The Instituto Nacional de Antropología e Historia (INAH) excavation of a mammoth mandible from an arroyo bank near Nochixtlán (site N 411) and the Vanderbilt University work at a dry cave (site N 221) near Yucuita yielded no substantial evidence of human activity for the Preceramic period.

Surveys and excavations conducted to date in the Mixteca Alta have focused primarily on Formative, Classic, Postclassic, and Colonial remains. No special effort has been devoted to the discovery or excavation of preceramic or incipient agricultural sites. Brockington's (Brockington, Jorrin, and Long 1974; Brockington and Long 1974) surveys on the Mixteca Costa, Moser's (1977) investigations in the Mixteca Baja, and Spores's surveys of other areas of the Mixteca Alta have provided no evidence of Preceramic or earliest agricultural sites. MacNeish (personal communication) located, but did not excavate, some promising caves on the road between Huajuapan and Tehuacán. The early cultigens identified from archaeological remains in the Nochixtlán Valley (C. E. Smith 1976) are like those recovered outside the Mixteca, and would appear to have evolved in other areas.

Preceramic sites undoubtedly exist in the Mixteca Baja, Alta, and Costa. The position of the Mixteca and its relationship to the Oaxaca and Tehuacán valleys during the Preceramic period and the era of agricultural incipience will remain in doubt until an appropriate research program similar to those mounted in Tehuacán and Oaxaca is conducted in the Mixteca.

TOPIC 6
Tentative Chronological Phases for the Oaxaca Preceramic

KENT V. FLANNERY

Thus far we have presented only a series of stratigraphic components and living floors from Preceramic sites in Oaxaca. We are now faced with the task of dividing those into tentative chronological phases, which can then be related to developments in Tehuacán and elsewhere. Our original

hope was that we could use the phase names already published for Tehuacán by MacNeish (1964, 1967b). Our materials are not sufficiently similar to permit this, though we do have significant artifactual cross-ties to Tehuacán during some periods.

TABLE 2.2
Tentative Chronological Phases for the Oaxaca Preceramic, with Characteristic Projectile Points, Flora, and Settlement Type for Each Component

Tentative phases	Site and level	Projectile point types	Important flora	Type of settlement and season[a]
Martínez (± 2000 B.C.)	Yuzanú Martínez Shelter, Upper B	None Virtually None		MRC (microband), dry? Multiple short-term occupations
Blanca (3300–2800 B.C.)	Cueva Blanca C	Coxcatlán, La Mina, Trinidad, Hidalgo		HCC (microband), winter
	Cueva Blanca D	Tilapa, La Mina, Trinidad, San Nicolás		HCC (microband), winter
Jícaras (5000–4000 B.C.)	Gheo-Shih A, B	Pedernales, La Mina, Trinidad, San Nicolás	*Zea* pollen	OAC (macroband), summer?
Naquitz (8900–6700 B.C.)	Guilá Naquitz B	Pedernales	Cucurbit seeds	Family microband, fall
	Guilá Naquitz C	None	*Zea* pollen	Family microband, fall
	Guilá Naquitz D	None		Family microband, fall
	Guilá Naquitz E	Unfinished Lerma?		Family microband, fall
	Cueva Blanca E	Very few		HCC (microband), winter?
Late Pleistocene (10,000 B.C.)?	Cueva Blanca F	None		Burned, broken Pleistocene fauna

[a] MRC = Maguey roasting camp; HCC = hunting camp (in cave); OAC = open-air camp.

There are four lines of evidence that can be used to produce a tentative Preceramic chronology for the Valley of Oaxaca (Table 2.2). The first is the stratigraphic relationship of the various living floors in our sites. The second is the radiocarbon dates for those living floors, summarized in Table 2.1. The third is the sequence of diagnostic artifacts, especially projectile point types. The fourth is a pollen chronology worked out by James Schoenwetter and his associates for Preceramic sites in the Mitla area (Schoenwetter and Smith n.d.). While Schoenwetter's final results are not available at this writing, his preliminary results support the scheme presented here (personal communication; see also Schoenwetter 1974).

The reason we consider our phases to be "tentative" is that the number of sites and components is small; the number of time-sensitive artifacts is small; the various sites show functional and seasonal differences which influence the artifact inventory; some levels yielded no preserved pollen or radiocarbon samples; and there are numerous lacunae in the sequence.

LATE PLEISTOCENE

According to Schoenwetter, the sterile, weathered volcanic tuff deposits in Zone F of Cueva Blanca, Zone D of the Martínez Rock Shelter, and basal Guilá Naquitz all yield a pollen spectrum that reflects colder temperatures than today's climate. In Cueva Blanca F, this deposit includes

Pleistocene animals similar to the Early Ajuereado fauna from Tehuacán. We have simply designated this phase late Pleistocene.

NAQUITZ

Next comes a series of seven living floors, including Cueva Blanca E and Guilá Naquitz E, D, C, B3, B2, and B1, which can be placed in a single phase. Based on available radiocarbon dates, a span of 8900–6700 B.C. would not be unreasonable for this period. Projectile points are rare, with a possible unfinished Lerma point from Guilá Naquitz E and a single Pedernales point from Guilá Naquitz B. Utilized flakes and one-hand manos are typical artifacts. This phase is significant because Guilá Naquitz D (8750–7840 B.C.) contains our oldest *pepo*-like cucurbit seed; Guilá Naquitz zones B and C (7450–6670 B.C.) contain 14 seeds and peduncles identified as *Cucurbita pepo*, as well as pollen grains of *Zea* cf. *mexicana* or teosinte (Flannery 1973:Table 2; Schoenwetter 1974; Whitaker n.d.). We have tentatively called this phase Naquitz.

It is impossible to correlate Naquitz precisely with the Tehuacán sequence. It contains only modern fauna, and therefore should be later than Early Ajuereado and Cueva Blanca F. Despite its modern fauna, however, it cannot be correlated with the El Riego phase in Tehuacán, which begins around 6800 B.C. and includes numerous projectile point types so far unknown from Naquitz. Johnson and MacNeish (1972:39–40 and Fig. 4) show Naquitz as being contemporaneous with Late Ajuereado in the Tehuacán Valley, but artifactually more like the Santa Marta phase from central Chiapas. We cannot add much, especially since the Late Ajuereado phase and the Naquitz phase have not, between them, produced enough time-sensitive diagnostic artifacts to allow us more precision.

JÍCARAS

The single Pedernales point from upper Guilá Naquitz was a harbinger of things to come. This projectile point type reached its major frequency during the phase which we have called Jícaras, after the type site of Gheo-Shih (*Río de las Jícaras*); it virtually disappeared before the occupation of Cueva Blanca D. Palynological data, as well as artifactual evidence, place Gheo-Shih somewhere midway between Guilá Naquitz B1 (6600 B.C.?) and Cueva Blanca D (3000 B.C.?). We have accordingly selected a date of 5000–4000 B.C. for Gheo-Shih, but cannot accurately date the beginning or end of the Jícaras phase. Significantly, Schoenwetter reports *Zea* pollen (either teosinte or primitive maize) from Gheo-Shih.

Jícaras is the first phase in the Oaxaca sequence in which projectile points occur in any abundance and variety. The most common point is the Pedernales type, a large-bladed atlatl point with moderate shoulders or barbs and a short, broad stem with a characteristic concave base (Figure 2.5). These points were evidently made by the hundreds in the eastern Valley of Oaxaca, but were never numerous in Tehuacán. MacNeish recovered a single Pedernales point (listed as an "aberrant" specimen) at the Level 4–3 transition in El Riego Cave West, "a component of the Coxcatlán phase" (MacNeish, Nelken-Terner, and Johnson 1967:78). The specimen they illustrate (Fig. 67) could easily be duplicated at Gheo-Shih. Level 4 of El Riego Cave West falls in the 4000 B.C. time range, within our estimate for Jícaras.

Other projectile points from Gheo-Shih include the contracting-stem types Trinidad and San Nicolás, and the straight-stemmed type La Mina (Figure 2.5). All three types are well represented during the 5000 to 4000 B.C. period at Tehuacán. The Jícaras phase remains also include metates and manos of various types, bifaces, choppers, scrapers of various kinds, stone ornaments, and utilized flakes (Hole n.d.).

BLANCA

Two levels at Cueva Blanca, Zones D and C, are sufficiently similar to be included within a tentative Blanca

phase. Zone D has produced radiocarbon dates in the 3295 to 2800 B.C. time range, coeval with the early-to-middle Abejas phase in the Tehuacán Valley. All the projectile point types from Cueva Blanca D and C are shared with Abejas sites in Tehuacán, though the frequencies are different. In Tehuacán, the distinctive Coxcatlán point is the most common type in the Abejas phase, while Trinidad, San Nicolás, and La Mina are less common. At Cueva Blanca, the proportions are reversed: San Nicolás, Trinidad, and La Mina are common, while Coxcatlán points are rare. Indeed, the two Coxcatlán points from Cueva Blanca are made of somewhat different raw material from our other points, and would not stand out if added to the collections from Coxcatlán Cave. Two other types from the Blanca phase, Tilapa and Hidalgo, have so far not been found in the earlier Jícaras phase (Figure 2.5).

Blanca is virtually the last phase in our sequence in which projectile points are common. This is an important contrast with the Tehuacán sequence, where projectile points remained common right up to the Spanish Conquest. In Oaxaca, the use of chipped-stone points declined rapidly after approximately 2500 B.C., and by the Formative they were decidedly rare.

If poorly known, the Blanca phase is at least widespread in the central highlands of Oaxaca. Ronald Spores (personal communication, 1975) reports the surface find of a Coxcatlán point from the slopes of Yucuñudahui in the Nochixtlán Valley. Tilapa points have been found on the valley floor between Tlacolula and Mitla. And in the Valley of Miahuatlán, 80 km south of Oaxaca, Donald Brockington (1973:15) reports a Trinidad point from Site 3 of his surface survey. Additional points from localities all over the Valley of Oaxaca, now in the collections of the Frissell Museum of Zapotec Art in Mitla, indicate that the hunters and "incipient cultivators" of the Blanca phase were wide-ranging, if not particularly numerous.

MARTÍNEZ

We come now to the latest, least securely dated, and most tentative phase in the Preceramic sequence. The Martínez phase is represented only by material from the upper 10 cm of Zone B at the Martínez Rock Shelter, which we have tentatively grouped with the Yuzanú material from the Yanhuitlán–Nochixtlán Valley. Yuzanú has produced radiocarbon dates of 2100 to 2000 B.C. (±200), but the material could easily go back to the 2300 B.C. date arbitrarily selected by Johnson and MacNeish (1972:24) for terminal Abejas. Indeed, since the oldest actual date for Purrón phase ceramics at Tehuacán is 1925 B.C. ±131 (Johnson and MacNeish 1972:25), even an estimate of 2100 to 2000 B.C. for terminal Abejas would not be out of the question.

The Martínez Rock Shelter does contain crude stone

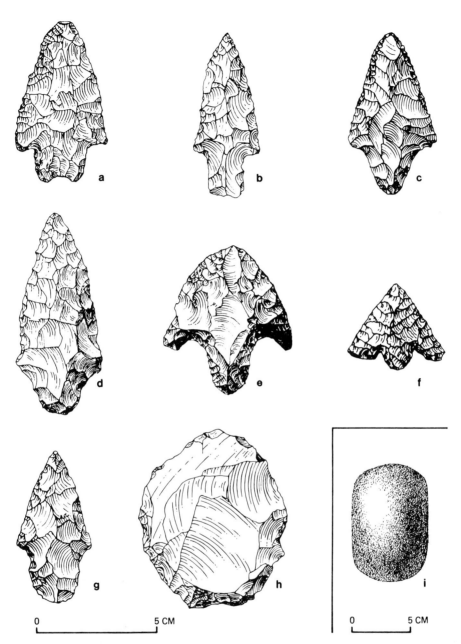

FIGURE 2.5. Artifacts used in the establishment of Preceramic chronological phases in Oaxaca: (a) Pedernales point; (b) La Mina point; (c) Trinidad point; (d) San Nicolás point; (e) Tilapa point; (f) Coxcatlán point; (g) Hidalgo point; (h) Martínez biface; (i) one-hand mano.

"bowls" (and/or mortars) which may be related to late Abejas phase specimens from Tehuacán. We are severely handicapped, however, by the near absence of projectile points from the Martínez Rock Shelter and their total absence at Yuzanú. A single La Mina point from the talus slope of the Martínez Rock Shelter suggests continuity from the Blanca phase, but by this time projectile points were becoming rare in Oaxaca. La Mina points were also rare during the Abejas

phase in Tehuacán, and unknown during the subsequent Purrón phase.

Perhaps the safest position to take would be to regard Martínez simply as the "last gasp" of the Preceramic in Oaxaca—possibly even overlapping slightly with the first introduction of ceramics—and to point out that two major activities were the grinding and pounding of vegetable foods and the baking of maguey hearts.

TOPIC 7
Ritual and Ceremonial Development at the Hunter–Gatherer Level

ROBERT D. DRENNAN

Before considering the evidence for ritual or ceremonial activity during the Preceramic period, I should clarify what I have taken to be included under the term *ritual* for the purposes of this volume. Definitions of ritual activity (which is not here distinguished from ceremonial activity) often focus on the repetition of an activity conducted in a precisely defined manner. In addition, a sense of appropriateness to a particular context is often included as a criterion. This sense of appropriateness is difficult to define precisely, but it involves the notion that certain circumstances call for a particular kind of ritual response, and that its absence would be felt as an omission in a peculiarly noninstrumental way. Ritual activities are symbolic. As such, one of their most important aspects is that they are communication events. In their context information is transmitted, although as Rappaport (1971a:63, 74) and others have pointed out, sometimes the sender and the receiver of the information are the same.

The attributes of ritual activity just cited can be taken to include an enormous variety of human behavior from a military salute (or its civilian analogue, a smile and a wave) to a Roman Catholic Mass to a presidential inauguration. All these activities are highly patterned, are often repeated, are extremely appropriate (to the point of being essential) in particular circumstances, and transmit information.

The patterning and the definition of appropriate circumstances for rituals are determined by sets of beliefs, and the failure to perform a ritual in the prescribed manner or when the appropriate circumstances arise implies an attack on the set of beliefs concerned. Each of the three examples of ritual cited in the previous paragraph involves a different set of beliefs. A salute or a wave is called for by beliefs concerning relations among individuals, a Roman Catholic Mass by religious beliefs, and a presidential inauguration by political or ideological beliefs. All three rituals are important to the society in which they occur, partly for reasons explicit in the belief systems which prescribe them and partly for other reasons. Rituals in general are important to the societies that support them because of the direct results of their performance as well as the transmission of information they accomplish.

Of the various kinds of belief sets that call for ritual activity, perhaps the most important is the set of religious beliefs. Rappaport (1971a; 1971b) has presented an argument for the connection of ritual, especially ritual that communicates certain kinds of socially important information, to religious beliefs. Elsewhere I have elaborated this argument with specific reference to Formative period Mesoamerica (Drennan 1976a). In very brief summary, rituals of special social importance are especially likely to be governed by religious beliefs because religious beliefs are especially effective in ensuring the proper performance of rituals. Thus the direct effects of the ritual activity are most to be depended upon if the ritual is religious. The information transmitted by a ritual is also most readily accepted if the ritual is religious. Thus a connection between socially important rituals and religious beliefs is a very successful solution to certain kinds of problems of social organization. Those interested in pursuing this line of reasoning may do so in the articles referred to above. For the present I simply note it, because together with the well-known difficulty of separating secular and sacred in primitive societies, it explains the religious slant to this discussion of ritual activity. The rituals discussed here are those deemed of particular social importance and for which we have at least a shred of evidence.

Unfortunately, the small amount of evidence available makes it impossible to present any rigorous or detailed reconstructions of ritual at the hunter–gatherer level. The following, then, is largely speculation based upon general consideration of the social roles of ritual and upon ethnographically known hunter–gatherer societies. As such it must not be taken as an established reconstruction of ritual among Mesoamerican hunter–gatherers, but rather as a set of propositions that, we hope, can be tested as further data become available. If some of these propositions can be confirmed it will show that some kinds of ritual practiced in better-documented later periods have roots stretching well back into the preagricultural past.

At the Preceramic open-air site of Gheo-Shih in the Valley of Oaxaca, Frank Hole excavated two parallel rows of boulders about 20 m long and 7 m apart, bounding an area that had been swept almost completely clean of artifacts (Flannery [ed.] 1970:23–24). Flannery has suggested that this feature, dating between 5000 and 4000 B.C., resembles the "dance grounds" reported for macroband camps of some Great Basin hunter–gatherers, whose dances took place in flat open areas in or adjacent to their camps. Sometimes these areas were defined by enclosures of posts and brush; sometimes they were unbounded or only partially bounded (Lowie 1915, 1924a:299). The dances were sometimes completely secular affairs but at other times were distinctly religious in nature (Lowie 1915, 1924a:301; Steward 1938:237). The consistent feature was that they were held at times when an unusually large number of people could gather together (Steward 1938). Sometimes this meant the inclusion of most or all members of a single band, and often members of other bands were invited to participate.

Steward has noted that the dances and the festivals of which they were a part "enhanced band solidarity." Lowie (1924a:809) indicates that in at least some cases particular dances were associated with particular bands. The bonds between members of the band were strengthened by participation, and contacts were maintained with other bands as well (Steward 1938:170). Courting and marriages sometimes occurred in the context of a dance (Reed 1896:244). Contexts in which such contact between bands occurred were rare. Thus these ritual activities had great social importance in regulating both the internal and external relations of the hunter–gatherer bands, which were fragmented into much smaller units during most of the year.

That any social group requires mechanisms for defining and solidifying itself has been accepted since before Durkheim (1912) emphasized the role of ritual in the process. Clearly these requirements apply to early Mesoamerican hunter–gatherers, and part of their fulfillment may have come from rituals such as those which seem to have occurred at Gheo-Shih when rainy season resources permitted the gathering of an unusually large number of people. Yengoyan (1972) has discussed the role such rituals may play in maintaining contacts among a number of such local groups ultimately extending over an extremely large geographical area. Facilitating contacts between groups is particularly difficult when population densities are as low as those which probably obtained at the hunter–gatherer level in Mesoamerica. The biological requirements of maintaining a successful breeding population would have encouraged regular contact among groups spread over a substantial area. That early Mesoamerican hunter–gatherers maintained either direct or indirect contact with distant regions is indicated by the presence of marine shell beads in the Tehuacán Valley by about 5000 B.C. during the El Riego phase (MacNeish, Nelken-Terner, and Johnson 1967:147). By Abejas phase times (3400–2300 B.C.), obsidian from outside the Tehuacán Valley was also being brought there for the manufacture of stone tools (MacNeish, Nelken-Terner, and Johnson 1967:11). If rituals such as those which seem to have occurred at Gheo-Shih involved the participation of several bands, they could have facilitated the transport of such materials.

Most of the remaining evidence for ritual at the hunter–gatherer level in Mesoamerica comes not from either the Mixtec or Zapotec regions, but from the Tehuacán Valley. The presence of elaborate burial ritual by about 5000 B.C. is indicated by the remains in Zone XIV of the El Riego phase in Coxcatlán Cave (MacNeish et al. 1972:266–270). Five individuals were buried in two separate burial events, during each of which several individuals were buried at approximately, if not exactly, the same time. One of these burial events involved two young children who had been beheaded and had their skulls exchanged. One of the skulls was charred and scraped. A number of baskets were included with the burials. A short distance away were found the burials of a very young child, an adult male, and an adult female with evidence that the remains were intentionally burned before the burial pit was filled in. Disarticulation and evidence of burning inside the mandible suggested to the excavators that the female adult was beheaded. Disarticulated

and very incomplete samples of burned and sometimes chopped human bone have been found in other Preceramic sites in Tehuacán (MacNeish et al. 1972:24–26, 82–84, 86–88). These samples indicate that rituals involving burning and cutting up of the deceased were not uncommon, although one complete burial in Zone R of Purrón Cave—dating between 6300 and 5400 B.C., during the El Riego phase (MacNeish et al. 1972:78–80)—shows that such rituals did not always follow death. The exact social roles expressed by the variety of burial rituals demonstrated cannot even be guessed because of the small number of examples. If and when more Preceramic burials are found, it may be possible to establish some pattern to the activities.

Of interest at the present, however, is the suggestion that at least some of the individuals involved in the Coxcatlán Cave burials may have been put to death in order to be buried, rather than dying of natural causes. As the excavators noted, it seems unlikely that the members of these two groups of individuals would die naturally at the same time, yet they were all buried at the same time. Moreover, decapitation and the kind of treatment to which some of the skulls were subjected are quite understandable in terms of a ritual in which some of the individuals were killed.

If such practices were at all common (and the overwhelming majority of human remains recovered from the Preceramic in Tehuacán indicate at least the possibility of such practices), they might have had some effect on population dynamics. While population estimates for the Preceramic are only guesses (see Topic 8), it does seem clear that the rate of population growth was considerably below that which is biologically possible. A high rate of ritual involving human sacrifice might certainly have contributed to this situation. In this context, it would be especially interesting to know under what circumstances such rituals were deemed appropriate. The plant and animal remains from Zones XIV and XV of Coxcatlán Cave reflect occupation in the late wet and early dry seasons, and MacNeish et al. (1972:267) believe the burials were interred during the dry season. If the rituals were associated with plant harvests (early dry season) or alternatively during a time of food scarcity (late dry season), then they were very adaptively connected to some of the important environmental variables relevant to population.

Historical sources document the practice of human sacrifice at the time of the Spanish Conquest, and it has been argued that it was carried out on a large enough scale to have an important effect on population size and growth rate (Cook 1946). The evidence from the Preceramic suggests that such rituals had a very long tradition behind them in Mesoamerica.

Two of the aspects of ritual mentioned at the beginning of this discussion are of particular importance to archaeologists: repetitiveness and rigid patterning. These two features imply that in the material remains of ritual activity one can observe a regularity lacking in the remains of unique events or of events occurring in a less rigidly prescribed manner. Despite this regularity, actual evidence of ritual among preagricultural peoples of Mesoamerica is quite rare—although perhaps not unexpectedly so in light of the general scarcity of data concerning these early periods. Thus most of the ritual activity speculated about is demonstrated by only slight evidence. It is impossible to prove, even if the speculations about the nature of the activities are at least partially accurate, that they were repeated. If they were not, they clearly do not merit discussion as ritual. This situation can only be remedied when the corpus of data concerning the Preceramic has been vastly increased.

TOPIC 8
Settlement, Subsistence, and Social Organization of the Proto-Otomangueans

KENT V. FLANNERY

We have reviewed the empirical data from excavation, proposed a series of chronological phases, and considered the evidence for ritual behavior among the Indians of Preceramic Oaxaca and Tehuacán. To go further, we must continue to increase our sample by combining our data with those of the Tehuacán Valley (MacNeish 1964, 1972). Bracketed as it is by the Mazatec region on the east and the Chocho–Popoloca region on the west, Tehuacán lies well within the area where Proto-Otomanguean should once have been spoken. In this topic I will briefly attempt to synthesize our data on settlement, subsistence, and social organization between 8000 and 2000 B.C.

SETTLEMENT

MacNeish (1964, 1972) originally distinguished two kinds of settlements in Tehuacán: "macroband" camps, occupied for a season or more by 15–25 persons, and "micro-band" camps, occupied by two to five individuals for any period from a day or two to most of a season. Since even microband camps may contain both men's and women's tools, the inference is that they were produced by family collecting bands like those of the Paiute or Shoshone (Steward 1955); macroband camps would then represent places where several families coalesced during a time of abundant resources. These settlements can be further divided by site function to produce a wider range of site types: hunting camps, plant collecting camps, maguey roasting camps, and so on (Figure 2.6).

Gheo-Shih would be an example of a macroband camp in the Valley of Oaxaca; as such it would be the functional equivalent of the Coxcatlán Cave and Terrace in the Tehuacán Valley. Gheo-Shih covers 1.5 ha and might have been occupied by 25 persons, probably during June–July–August when the surrounding mesquite groves would have been heavy with pods (180–200 kg. of edible portion per hectare), and when rainy-season cultivation of

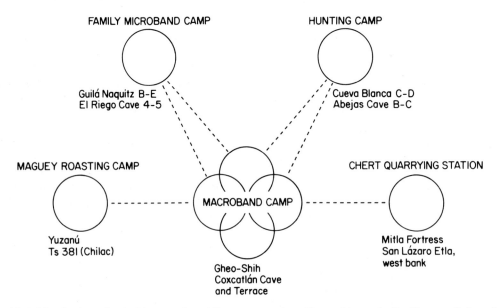

FIGURE 2.6. Model for the hypothetical integration of five preceramic settlement types in the Oaxaca–Tehuacán area. Each circle represents a "microband" (in MacNeish's terminology). Two actual archaeological examples of each settlement type are given.

early domestic plants could take place. There are oval concentrations of rocks and tools that may indicate residence in small shelters; if so, these were apparently without postholes, and their floors were not excavated into the ground. We have already mentioned the boulder-lined dance ground in the center of the site and the ornament-making area (Topic 5). These areas suggest that certain rituals and craft activities may have been deferred until the local group was united in a macroband camp.

With the breakup of a macroband camp like Gheo-Shih, individual families evidently spread out over the countryside to engage in a wide range of activities. Zones E-B1 at Guilá Naquitz Cave would be examples of another settlement type, the microband camp whose primary purpose was for wild plant collecting. Guilá Naquitz was probably occupied by only three to five persons, beginning at the end of the mesquite harvest season (September?) and lasting until the end of the acorn harvest (December?). In the Tehuacán Valley, Zones 5–4 of El Riego Cave would be examples of this same settlement type.

Other microband camps seem to have been oriented more strongly toward hunting, although this was probably a difference of degree rather than kind. Zones D–C at Cueva Blanca reflect this kind of microband occupation, with projectile points and deer bones relatively well represented and grinding implements rare. In the Tehuacán Valley, Zones C–B of Abejas Cave represent this kind of hunting-oriented microband camp.

In the heart of the dry season (February) there are too few plants available in the Guilá Naquitz area to keep a family alive, and often the deer have moved up to the higher mountains where the lower evapotranspiration provides them with more to browse on. One of the activities of this season is the roasting of *Agave* hearts, which are available year-round. I believe that one example of a maguey-roasting camp would be Yuzanú near Yanhuitlán. In the Tehuacán Valley, the west half of site Ts 381 near Chilac has a maguey-roasting pit, assigned by MacNeish and García Cook (1972:157) to the El Riego phase. I expect most (but not all) maguey-roasting camps to date to the dry season and to be found at elevations above the valley floor.

Still another site type of this period, not considered a true camp, is the flint or chert quarry. Surface finds of preforms and unfinished projectile points indicate that the slopes of the so-called Mitla fortress (see Topic 88) provided chert-like silicified tuff for Preceramic knappers. So did the limestone outcrops of Yucuñudahui, a high mountain in the Nochixtlán Valley. Another quarry is a chert outcrop near San Lázaro Etla on the west bank of the Atoyac River north of Oaxaca City. These sites would have been visited periodically as raw material was needed.

Settlement systems of the Preceramic era must have been flexible and dynamic, allowing family collecting bands to spread out as far as possible when resources were scarcest and to converge on a favored camp ground when resources were most abundant. It would be a mistake, however, to assume a simple correlation between macrobands and the rainy season, microbands and the dry season. In a bumper year for mesquite, the macroband coalescence might take place on the alluvium in July; in a bumper year for acorns, it might take place in the upper piedmont during November. During a drought year, there might never be an opportunity for macroband settlement. Thus, certain rituals were probably ad hoc and time-independent, occurring at times of unpredictable surplus (Flannery 1972a).

I suggest that all these settlement types could occur in caves or out in the open, the latter being less frequently excavated but probably more common. Our data from Gheo-Shih suggest that some open-air sites might have had small oval shelters or windbreaks. On the east side of Ts 381 near Chilac in the Tehuacán Valley, MacNeish and García Cook (1972:156–60) report a "pit house" dating to the Abejas phase. Since I have elsewhere argued that it would be premature to conclude there were Abejas phase "villages" or "hamlets" on the basis of this single excavated feature (Flannery 1972b:37–38), I will not repeat the argument here. Hunters and gatherers the world over build shelters, huts, and windbreaks on their camps (Fraser 1968), and no one calls them villages. I expect that as more sites like Gheo-Shih and Ts 381 are excavated, we will find an even wider range of shelter types on them. We will probably also find that we do not have an adequate terminology to convey the diversity of settlement types in the late Preceramic.

SUBSISTENCE

I have already discussed hunting, gathering, and incipient agriculture in two previous articles (Flannery 1968a, 1973), so there is no need to spend much time on it here. I will simply review the evidence as it stood on the eve of the Santa Fe seminar in 1975.

The whole of the region within which the Proto-Otomangueans are thought to have lived would originally have been forested mountains and brush-covered valleys. At 1000-m elevation, in the arid tropical thorn forest around Coxcatlán Cave in the Tehuacán Valley, plant collectors would have had access to fruits of the *chupandilla* (*Cyrtocarpa procera*), *cozahuico* (*Sideroxylon* sp.), buckthorn (*Condalia mexicana*), *susí* (*Jatropha neopauciflora*), and possibly wild avocado (*Persea americana*); seeds of foxtail grass (*Setaria* sp.); *Agave* and prickly pear (*Opuntia* spp.); organ cactus fruits of several species; and pods of the *pochote* (*Ceiba parvifolia*) and *guaje* (*Leucaena* sp.). At 1500 m, on the Oaxaca Valley floor near Gheo-Shih, there would have been pods of mesquite (*Prosopis* sp.) and fruits of the hackberry (*Celtis* sp.). At 1900 m, in Thorn Forest A near Guilá Naquitz, there would have been acorns, piñon nuts, *susí*, *guaje*, *Agave*, prickly pear, nanche, wild onion, and all the species mentioned on page 21. The still-higher Yanhuitlán–Nochixtlán Valley (2100 m) would have had oak–pine forest with nearby mountain resources like black walnuts (*Juglans* sp.) and wild black zapote (*Diospyros* sp.).

While most foodstuffs come from near the site, Preceramic foragers did not hesitate to make climbs of 1000 m elevation; thus, a few acorns from the oak zone appeared at 975 m in Coxcatlán Cave (C. E. Smith 1967:239).

Just as varied as the diet were the other economic uses of plants by these Preceramic foragers. The inflorescence of the *lechuguilla* (*Hechtia* sp.), soft and punky, served as the "hearth" for a fire-drill made from harder wood. Maguey and *Tillandsia* fibers were extracted to make cordage for carrying bundles; the finest fibers were used to make snares for birds and small game. Oak leaves, grass, and *pochote* floss were used as soft bedding in caves. Wooden tongs were used to remove cactus fruits from the stem, or to move glowing coals around in a hearth. Canes (*Phragmites communis*) were used as projectile mainshafts.

The white-tailed deer was the principal quarry of the Proto-Otomanguean hunter; peccary were less frequently killed. Cottontails and jackrabbits were the principal small mammals eaten, with opossums, raccoons, foxes, pocket gophers, ground squirrels, pack rats, and even skunks taken on occasion. Quail, doves, and pigeons were the most common birds in the diet. Mud turtles, snakes, and lizards were eaten, and at lower elevations so were black and green iguanas. The domestic dog is known from at least Abejas phase times (Flannery 1967).

Sometime between the end of the Pleistocene and 5000 B.C., the first steps toward agriculture were taken by these ancient hunter–gatherers. Donald Lathrap (personal communication) has suggested that the bottle gourd (*Lagenaria*) may have been the first New World plant domesticated because of its obvious utility to Preceramic food collectors. This suggestion is not unreasonable, though it cannot at the moment be confirmed or denied; if confirmed, it provides a hypothesis for the whole history of cucurbit domestication. Bottle gourd rinds occur in Zones C–B of Guilá Naquitz Cave (7400–6700 B.C.) in association with 14 seeds and peduncles of the "squash," *Cucurbita pepo*[1]. It may be that squashes were originally domesticated by hunter–gatherers who already knew and cultivated the bottle gourd and who therefore instantly recognized these other members of the cucurbit family as potentially useful when they ran across them (Flannery 1973:301).

Indeed, the tendency of most cucurbits to be "weedy camp followers" (Cutler and Whitaker 1967), which do well on disturbed soils like the talus slope of an occupied cave, probably encouraged their domestication. Between 5000 and 3000 B.C., two more cucurbits, *C. mixta* and *C. moschata*, appeared in Tehuacán Valley sites (Cutler and Whitaker 1967). Both Guilá Naquitz and El Riego Cave also included

specimens of the wild coyote melon *Apodanthera* sp. As cucurbits which become "tolerated weed associate[s] of man prior to the practice of agriculture" may already show "an increase in seed size over most wild species" (Cutler and Whitaker 1967), we may never know the exact date of domestication for each species.

The situation with beans is even more complicated. Hundreds of small, wild black runner beans were harvested by the occupants of Guilá Naquitz between 8700 and 6700 B.C., but the species (which still grows near the cave) is one that has never been domesticated (Lawrence Kaplan, personal communication 1970). Common beans (*Phaseolus vulgaris*) are not known from Tehuacán until 4000–3000 B.C. levels, while tepary beans (*Phaseolus acutifolius*) are abundant by 3000 B.C. (Kaplan 1967); neither appears at Guilá Naquitz.

As for the appearance of maize in the Otomanguean region, I have little to add to the model I presented in the *Annual Review of Anthropology* (Flannery 1973). Pollen grains of the genus *Zea*, in the size range of those of teosinte (*Z. mexicana*), occur in 7400 to 6700 B.C. levels at Guilá Naquitz (Schoenwetter 1974). The outstanding recent genetic and anatomical research of Walton Galinat (1970, 1971) suggests that maize is ultimately derived from teosinte, a view shared by George Beadle, Jack Harlan, and others; Paul Mangelsdorf (1974) still disagrees. Eighteen cobs of undeniable maize (*Zea mays*) occur in a 5050 B.C. level at Coxcatlán Cave. Mangelsdorf considers them wild, while Galinat (1971) argues that they "can also be interpreted as in the early stages of transformation of teosinte to maize," that is, domesticated. By the time of the Abejas phase in the Tehuacán Valley (3400–2300 B.C.) and the Blanca phase in the Valley of Oaxaca (3300–2800 B.C.), domesticated corn was probably as widespread in the Otomanguean region as Coxcatlán projectile points.

SOCIAL ORGANIZATION

It goes without saying that we have no concrete data on the social or territorial organization of the Preceramic hunter–gatherers of the Otomanguean region. I feel, however, that we must attempt to draw some inferences about these topics, since this period forms the baseline for all subsequent sociocultural evolution among the Cloud People.

One of the variables affecting the social organization of the hunting-gathering bands is low population density. The highest density reported for any band-level hunter–gatherer group is three persons per mi² on the Andaman Islands; the lowest is one person per 300 mi² for the Naskapi of Labrador (Okada 1954). Most densities probably fell within the narrower estimate of Julian Steward (1955:125), "ranging from a maximum which seldom exceeds one person per 5 square miles to one person per 50 or more square miles" (Fried 1967:55).

First, let us see how the Tehuacán data fit with these fig-

---

[1]The species *Cucurbita pepo* today includes "the common New England pumpkin, White Bush Scallop squash, Zucchini squash, Summer Crookneck squash, and Acorn squash" (Cutler and Whitaker 1967:212). Thus, while it has been common practice to refer to it as a pumpkin in the archaeological literature, I feel this practice should be discouraged because it conjures up a misleading image. The *Cucurbita pepo* of 7400 B.C. had a small, yellowish fruit the size of an orange, which in no way resembled the familiar Halloween pumpkin.

ures. MacNeish (1964:531) gives the area of his survey as 70 by 20 miles, for a total of 140 square miles. His map of El Riego phase sites (MacNeish 1972:Fig. 3) shows 7 macroband camps[2] and 13 microband camps from the entire 2000-year span of the phase. Remembering that microband camps are simply the lean-season settlements of the same people who lived at macroband camps during the high-resource seasons, we include only the macroband camps in our calculations. MacNeish has elsewhere estimated that macrobands consisted of 15 to 25 persons. If we assume that all 7 camps were occupied simultaneously (a very unlikely situation), we have a population of 105 to 175 persons in 140 square miles, or about 1 person per square mile. Making the more likely assumption that the 7 camps represent a series of settlements occupied sequentially over a 2000-year period, we could have as few as 0.1–0.2 persons per square mile. This would translate to one person per 5–10 square miles, near the upper end of Steward's range, and this is the estimate I prefer.

In fact, this range of figures illustrates the difficulty of estimating hunter–gatherer populations from archaeological data. Even the finest of macroband camps were occupied for only "two or more seasons" (MacNeish 1972:75). Thus a macroband of 25 persons who moved their settlement every year could, along with their descendants, leave behind 2000 macroband camps during the El Riego phase alone. An archaeologist locating 7 of these would have recovered 0.4% of the macroband camps of that period. In a sample that size, the chances that he would recover two sites occupied in the same year, let alone simultaneously, are extremely small. The chances that all 7 were occupied simultaneously should be close to zero. For these reasons, we believe it would be premature for us to draw lines around "band territories" as MacNeish (1972) has done in his Figs. 3, 4, and 5. While his 7 macroband camps do occur in 3 clusters, we have no reason to believe they were occupied simultaneously by neighboring bands. Such is the nature of Preceramic sites that "clusters" are more likely to represent favorable survey areas where old land surfaces are exposed, or where there are suitable cave formations.

For much the same reasons, we do not believe the data will support a hypothesis of population growth during Preceramic times, either in Tehuacán or Oaxaca. For the Abejas phase, MacNeish (1972:Fig. 5) recovered 10 macroband camps and "central bases" occupied during an 1100-year phase—slightly less than 1% of the potential number of macroband camps left by a group of 25 persons and their descendants. Thus, by comparing the "population" of the El Riego phase with that of the Abejas phase we might be comparing an 0.4% sample with an 0.9% sample; it is unlikely the differences would be significant.

If anything, the situation is even more speculative in the Valley of Oaxaca. Out of a sample of more than 50 caves we

visited, no more than half a dozen gave any evidence of Preceramic occupation. While stray Preceramic artifacts are not uncommon on the surface in the Mitla area, only at Gheo-Shih was there enough depth of deposit to give us an open-air site we could actually excavate. If we assume that Gheo-Shih was occupied by a macroband of 25 persons whose "territory" was the eastern half of the Tlacolula Valley, there might have been no more than 50 persons in the entire Tlacolula arm of the Valley of Oaxaca during the Jícaras phase. Extrapolation from this would give us 150 persons in the entire 700 km² of the Valley of Oaxaca, or 1 person per 4.7 km² of valley floor (i.e., 1 per 1.7 mi²). If we assume, however, that each arm of the Valley of Oaxaca had only 1 macroband of 25 persons, for a total population of 75, we would have 1 person per 9 km² (i.e., 1 per 3 square miles).

We thus have estimates ranging from as high as 1 per mi² (Tehuacán) and 1 per 1.7 mi² (Oaxaca) to as low as 1 per 5–10 mi² (Tehuacán) and 1 per 3 mi² (Oaxaca). The lower figures, for which I have already stated my preference, are more like those of the Great Basin Indians on whose ethnographic description (Steward 1938, 1955) MacNeish has often relied in constructing his Tehuacán models. If we round them off in the metric system which will be used throughout this volume, it gives us a range of 1 person per 9–29 km². And this figure includes only the valley areas, not the surrounding mountains.

Microband camp data suggest that the smallest group that ever resided together was the nuclear family, perhaps 2–5 people. Five to 10 of these families might coalesce into a group of about 25, which apparently constituted the local band, the largest number of people who ever lived together in a macroband camp. Twenty-five is, of course, the magic number which shows up over and over again in the ethnographic literature as the modal size for a local hunter–gatherer group with a generalized plant–animal diet (Birdsell 1968:235). Such a group "must be large enough to function successfully in a social sense, and small enough to minimize strain of food and water resources" (Birdsell 1968:235).

There would, however, have to have been two larger units to which these local groups belonged: the effective breeding population and the dialect tribe. In a recent simulation of hunter–gatherer population dynamics, Wobst (1974) concluded that 175–475 persons was the minimum pool needed to assume that all persons, over several generations, would find mates outside their circle of relatives. Birdsell (1968:239), for his part, has estimated that the effective breeding population might be as low as 175 for dialect tribes with a modal value of 500. As for the dialect tribe—all those people essentially speaking the same mutually intelligible language—among hunters and gatherers with generalized diets, "its numbers tend to stabilize around a population involving 500 individuals, quite independently of population density, the richness of the biota, and the technological development of extractive efficiency" (Birdsell 1968:239). In other words, there might have been a time, far back in the

---

[2]The conflict between MacNeish's text ("eleven macrobands") and map (7 macrobands) results from the fact that there were a total of 11 *levels* at the 7 *localities*.

Preceramic, when Proto-Otomanguean was a dialect spoken by 500 hunter-gatherers in the southern Mexican highlands.

Whatever the case, the arguments of Birdsell and Wobst have implications for the ancesters of the Cloud People. Given our population estimates, none of the valleys we have considered—Oaxaca, Nochixtlán, or Tehuacán—would have had enough people to constitute a self-contained breeding population, much less a dialect tribe. It would have taken 15 local groups such as the one encamped at Gheo-Shih to reach the minimum breeding pool calculated by Wobst, 20 such groups to reach the minimum dialect tribe calculated by Birdsell. Obviously,the local groups of all these valleys had to remain in sufficient contact with each other to exchange mates. That they also exchanged "gifts" is suggested by the two Coxcatlán points that showed up in Cueva Blanca, and the single Pedernales point that showed up in El Riego Cave. From the linguistic standpoint, this type of contact probably helped prevent Proto-Otomanguean from splitting into Proto-Zapotecan and Proto-Mixtecan branches prior to 4100 to 3700 B.C.

We might reconstruct the Preceramic hunter–gatherers of Oaxaca, therefore, as organized into *families* of 2 to 5 persons who harvested wild foods together at places like Guilá Naquitz, and in turn belonged to *local groups* averaging 25 related persons, all of whom might camp together at places like Gheo-Shih when resources permitted. These local groups would have been linked by marriage into an *effective breeding population* of 175 or more persons occupying neighboring valleys, and a still larger *dialect tribe* of at least 500 persons speaking Proto-Otomanguean.

As for the kinship system of 8900 to 2000 B.C., we have only the following suggestion to offer. The later Zapotec and Mixtec had a form of bilateral kinship classified as Hawaiian, combined with class-endogamous social strata (see Topic 95). We might expect their Preceramic ancestors to have had a simpler form of organization, without ranking or social strata, but possibly also bilateral. Many egalitarian American Indian societies (including hunter–gatherers like the Paiute and Shoshone) have variants of Hawaiian kinship. It allows for the existence of small, nuclear family collecting groups (i.e., microbands) on the one hand, and both kindreds and bilaterally extended families (i.e., macrobands) on the other; thus it would account for both the observed Preceramic settlement pattern and the presence of Hawaiian terms among the later Mixtec and Zapotec. An alternative possibility is the equally bilateral "Eskimo" kinship system, which can be converted to the Hawaiian type through some relatively simple changes in cousin terms (Murdock 1949: Table 73), and which features both independent nuclear families and kindreds. The Hawaiian type, however, is far more widespread in Mesoamerica.

TOPIC 9
The Cultural Legacy of the Oaxacan Preceramic

JOYCE MARCUS
KENT V. FLANNERY
RONALD SPORES

With this topic, we begin our attempt to outline some similarities and differences between the Zapotec and Mixtec. On the Preceramic level, there is really only one question we can ask: of the similarities shown by the Cloud People, which ones might be a legacy of their common ancestors, the Proto-Otomanguean hunter–gatherers?

TECHNOLOGY

The most obvious aspect of this legacy is technology. The Proto-Otomangueans already had the spear, the atlatl, the maguey-roasting pit, the basket, the net carrying bag, and all of the various grinding stones, tongs, snares, cordage, and equipment needed to live off the wild flora and fauna of their region. Much of this equipment continued in use not merely through the Spanish Conquest, but up to the present day.

One possible difference is that areas such as the Tehuacán Valley continued to use great numbers and varieties of flint and obsidian projectile points with their atlatl darts right through the Formative period, as did the Valleys of Puebla and Mexico (see MacNeish, Nelken-Terner, and Johnson 1967). In the Valley of Oaxaca, chipped-stone projectile points almost vanished at the end of the Preceramic era, just as they did in Chiapas to the south (Lowe 1959:75). This disappearance may be due to a shift in emphasis from use of the atlatl to use of the net for deer hunting during the Formative. The Chiapanec drove deer into large nets and dispatched them with wooden spears (Lowe 1959), and the Valley Zapotec may have done the same. Judging by one sixteenth-century dictionary (Córdova 1578a), the Zapotec had numerous terms for nets; there were "nets for deer (*quixechina*)," "nets for rabbits (*quixepillaana*)," "nets for pumas (*quixepeeche*)," "nets for fish (*quixepella*)," "nets for small black birds in the milpa (*quixepioxe*)," and so on.

The ancestral Proto-Otomanguean pattern seems to have been for hunting with atlatl darts tipped with stone points. A shift toward increased net-hunting and trapping at the end of the Preceramic would explain one of the first technological divergences we see in our region of study: continued abundance of projectile points in Formative Tehuacán and the northern Mixteca, decreasing numbers of projectile points in the Formative Valley of Oaxaca. However, the Zapotec retained the atlatl for warfare (see Topic 91).

PLANT AND ANIMAL CLASSIFICATION

We began this topic with technology because it is a relatively easy subject to deal with. We feel, however, that the legacy of the Preceramic went far beyond technology into the realm of world view, cosmology, and ethnoscience. The Preceramic era, after all, was one in which a great deal of the Indian's attention was focused on the wild plants and animals of his environment. To survive, he needed intimate knowledge of the habits and habitats of the animals, the seasonality and growth cycles of the plants. It stands to reason that this was the period during which the ancestors of the Zapotec and Mixtec originally worked out the basic principles for systematically classifying the plants and animals of their world. While we would never claim that such classificatory systems remained static for 10,000 years, it does seem possible that some basic principles have remained as a legacy of the hunting–gathering era. Our methodology for detecting these common principles is similar to glottochronology: where the sixteenth-century Zapotec and Mixtec classifications appear to be nearly identical, we consider it possible that they *were* identical before the separation of Proto-Zapotecan and Proto-Mixtecan. An alternative explanation—that the Mixtec derived their plant/animal classification from the Zapotec, or vice versa—we consider possible but less likely, given the conservative nature of this aspect of culture. In our examination of such "ethnoscientific" concerns, we have relied on both ethnohistoric documents and the two major sixteenth-century dictionaries: Fray Juan de Córdova (1578a) for the Zapotec, Fray Francisco de Alvarado (1593) for the Mixtec.

THE VITAL FORCE

It seems that both Mixtec and Zapotec based their classification on a fundamental distinction between living and nonliving matter. Among both peoples, the diagnostic characteristic of "living" matter and creatures was their possession of a kind of vital force or entelechy, which the sixteenth-century Spaniards found difficult to translate: *ánima, espíritu, lo que da vida* are various attempts at explanation. For the Zapotec, the vital force was something called *pèe*, variously translated as "wind," "breath," or "spirit." For the Mixtec, the equivalent concept was *yni* or *ini*, "spirit," "heart," and "heat." Thus the vital force was conceived of as making living things warm, of filling them with a kind of "sacred wind" that made them move; this vital force could occupy animate beings as well as some inanimate objects.

THE ANIMAL WORLD

The Zapotec divided animals (*mani*) into several broad categories, including animals walking on four legs (*mani tizaa cotaa*), aquatic animals (*mani niça*, from *niça*, "water"), and flying animals (*mani piguiñi*). Most names for animals began with a *pe* or *pi* sound, perhaps an animal classifier but just as likely a reflection of the fact that animals had *pèe* because they were alive. Animals were further divided into classes such as deer (*pichina*), cottontails (*peela*), jackrabbits (*pillaana*), and fish (*pella*), which might be divided into smaller categories by the use of an adjective. Wild animals were *mani quijxi*, roughly "animals of the *monte*."

The Mixtec also divided animals (*quete*) into those that walked on four legs (*quetesasican*), aquatic animals (*quetenohonduta*, from *duta*, "water"), and flying animals (*quetendahua*, from *andahui* or *andevui*, "sky"). Many animal names began with the *ti* or *te* sound, which the sixteenth-century Spaniards believed was an animal classifier derived from the contraction of *quete*. Some participants in the Santa Fe seminar, however, wondered if *ti* might not represent phonological change from *chi*, "wind." If so, both Mixtec *ti* and Zapotec *pèe* might ultimately derive from a common ancestral term for "wind" or vital force. Examples of Mixtec terms for specific animals would include *tiyaca* ("fish"), *tiyuhu* ("pocket gopher"), and *tioto* ("wild rat").

Both Zapotec and Mixtec words for "human being" began with sounds similar to their respective animal classifiers: *peni* for the Zapotec (*behn* in Mitla today) and *tay* for the Mixtec.

THE PLANT WORLD

Both the Zapotec and the Mixtec had a single word which simultaneously meant "plant," "tree," and "wood." For the sixteenth-century Zapotec, the word was *yaga;* for the sixteenth-century Mixtec, it was *yutnu*. Each language also had a word for "fruit," or "edible plant part," *nocuana* for the Zapotec and *cuihi* or *huihi* for the Mixtec. The sixteenth-century Zapotec referred to "flowers" as *quie, guije,* or *quije*, while the adjective *quijxi* was used to mean "wild," "weeds," "of the *monte*," or "not eaten," in the case of both plants and animals. The Mixtec term *ita* or *yta* was used for "flowers" or *yerba* (in the sense of "weeds").

These words could be combined, or used with modifiers, in order to specify different plants. The Zapotec divided woody vegetation into such categories as *yaga layna*, "trees which can be harvested," and *yaga quijxi* (literally "tree" + "wild" or "not eaten"); to specify "wilderness" or "dense wild vegetation" they used *quijxitao* ("weeds" + augmentative). The Mixtec equivalent of *quijxitao* was *saisi yta*, also using the term for "weeds." The Mixtec equivalent of *yaga layna* was *yutnu huihi*, "fruit tree." An inedible fruit was *cuihi dzonahaca* to the sixteenth-century Mixtec; to the Zapotec it was *picagaquixitani* ("acorn (?)" + "inedible plant" + "of the mountains").

Both the Zapotec and Mixtec could further specify plants by adding modifiers. For example, *yaga queti* specified a "pine tree" for the Zapotec, *yaga pichij* an "organ cactus." Further adjectives could be added to specify whether an organ cactus was *Lemaireocereus, Cephalocereus,* or *Myrtillocactus* (see Marcus and Flannery 1978).

THE SUPERNATURAL WORLD

When we shift our attention to the world of the supernatural, we see both significant similarities and some significant differences among the Zapotec and Mixtec. Both interacted with a series of great natural forces which moved and were therefore classified as being alive; wind, clouds, lightning, thunder, fire, and earthquakes figured in their ritual, sacred lore, and calendars. Unfortunately, the ritual aspects of Indian life were those least understood by the sixteenth-century Spaniards, making it all the more difficult to decide whether the similarities are later convergences or the legacy of a distant common ancestry.

For the Zapotec, the great natural forces commanded respect because they had *pèe.* Lightning (*cocijo*) split the clouds (*zaa*) and caused rain (*niça quije*) to descend; thunder was *xoo cocijo,* "lightning's earthquake." *Cocijo* was one of the most powerful natural forces, and the Zapotec frequently prayed, addressed, and sacrificed to *Pitao Cocijo,* an expression often invoked by the Zapotec which the sixteenth-century Spaniards erroneously translated as "the God of Rain" (Flannery and Marcus 1976b). From this error followed a number of misconceptions about Zapotec religion which Marcus discusses in Topic 97. In fact, *Pitao* is *pèe* + augmentative, and *Pitao Cocijo* is more accurately translated "Great Spirit (or Breath, or Wind) within the Lightning."

For the Mixtec, lightning (*tasa*) also split the clouds (*huico*) to release rain (*dzavui*), but thunder was *sacana dzavui;* its primary referent was to "rain" rather than to "lightning." This brings us to an interesting difference between Zapotec and Mixtec. Among the Cuicatec, the closest linguistic relatives of the Mixtec, *rayo* (Spanish) or "lightning" was a powerful supernatural, just as it was among the Zapotec (Hunt 1972:207). The same is true for the Maya, where *chac* (contrary to popular belief) refers to lightning, not rain.[1] All these terms suggest that during most ancient times in southern Mexico the feared and revered supernatural was lightning, whereas rain was just a form of water; among the Zapotec, for example, it was simply *niça quije,* "water from the sky." Among the Mixtec, however, *dzavui* ("rain") seems to have been the powerful supernatural, while "water" (*duta*) was a harmless substance that could be manipulated directly.

---

[1]See Marcus 1978:181, footnote 1.

Our suspicion is that on a Proto-Otomanguean level, it was lightning that was of major importance to several groups. If the Mixtec diverged from this pattern, it may not have been until after the linguistic separation of Cuicatec and Mixtec, which is glottochronologically estimated to be in the neighborhood of 2100–1300 B.C. (1700–1100 B.C. in radiocarbon years). Alternatively, the Mixtec emphasis on rain rather than on lightning might reflect their closer contact over the centuries with central Mexico, where Tlaloc appears to have been of paramount importance.

There are other similarities. For both Zapotec and Mixtec, "day" and "time" were the same word: *chij* for the Zapotec, *quehui* for the Mixtec. This may be another basic concept of great antiquity, as it is also true for the Maya. Then there are other contrasts. For the Mixtec, "fire," "earth," and "sacred" were all *ñuhu;* for the Zapotec, all three were very different words.

THE SHAPE OF THE COSMOS

When we reach the level of the cosmos, we find not only shared beliefs between the Mixtec and Zapotec, but also a set of structures which are virtually universal among Mesoamerican Indians. All believed that the universe was rectangular; that it was divided into four great world quarters; that each quarter was associated with a color, sometimes with a fifth color for the center; and that the main axis along which the cosmos was divided was the east–west path of the sun.

Among the sixteenth-century Valley Zapotec, for example, "east" was *çooche lani copijcha,* "where the sun rises"; "west" was *çootiace copijcha,* "where the sun sets" (Córdova 1578a). The four world quadrants were also associated with the four quarters of a day, and time moved clockwise from east (morning) to south (midday), then on to the west (afternoon) and north (night). Among the twentieth-century Isthmus Zapotec, "east" is *neza ridani gubidxa,* "road of the rising sun"; "west" is *neza riaazi gubidxa,* "road of the descending sun" (Pickett 1959).

Among the Mixtec, although the names for the directions "north" and "south" vary widely from one locale to another and are frequently based on regional landmarks, "east" is "where the sun rises," and "west" is "where the sun sets" (Mary Elizabeth Smith, personal communication). One sixteenth-century dictionary described 'east' as *sayo canandicandij,* "west" as *sayo caindicandij,* with the same translations given in the preceding sentence (Alvarado 1593). Actually, the situation was the same among the Maya, where *likin* or "east" referred to the rising sun, *chikin* or "west" to the setting sun.

As for the concept of color-related world quarters, it is so widespread among the Indians of North, Middle, and South America, as well as vast areas of Asia (see Nowotny 1970; Marcus 1970) as to suggest that it may have been part of the